The Alfred Hitchcock Quote Book

SAIL AT TEN
THIS PARTY NEEDS IS A LITTLE GLAND
WE'D BETTER START
HAVE TO BE ON
ONE WEEK IN
UP ALICIA
NINE.
LOWN OVER
THIS WHOLE
WILL BE
YOU LOVE ME

The
Alfred Hitchcock
Quote Book

Laurent Bouzereau

A Citadel Press Book
Published by Carol Publishing Group

I dedicate this book
to my family

A Citadel Press Book
Published by Carol Publishing Group
Citadel Press is a registered trademark of Carol Communications, Inc.
Editorial Offices: 600 Madison Avenue, New York, N.Y. 10022
Sales & Distribution Offices: 120 Enterprise Avenue, Secaucus, N.J.
   07094
In Canada: Canadian Manda Group, P.O. Box 920, Station U, Toronto,
   Ontario M8Z 5P9
Queries regarding rights and permissions should be addressed to
Carol Publishing Group, 600 Madison Avenue, New York, N.Y. 10022

Carol Publishing Group books are available at special discounts
for bulk purchases, for sales promotions, fund raising, or
educational purposes. Special editions can be created to specifications.
For details contact: Special Sales Department, Carol Publishing
Group, 120 Enterprise Avenue, Secaucus, N.J. 07094

Manufactured in the United States of America
10   9   8   7   6   5   4   3   2   1

Library of Congress Cataloging-in-Publication Data

Bouzereau, Laurent.
   The Alfred Hitchcock quote book / by Laurent Bouzereau.
      p.   cm.
   "A Citadel Press book."
   ISBN 0-8065-1390-X (paper)
      1. Hitchcock, Alfred, 1899-1980. —Quotations. 2. Hitchcock, Alfred,
   1899-1980. —Criticism and interpretations. I. Title.
PN 1998.3.H58B66   1933
791.43'0233'092—dc20   92-37554
                                                              CIP

Contents

ACKNOWLEDGMENTS

I wish to thank the following people who helped me with this book: My agent, Kay McCauley; my editor, Allan J. Wilson; my parents, Micheline and Daniel; my sisters, Géraldine and Cécile; and, in alphabetical order:

Charles Bennett, Stuart Birnbaum, Merrick Bursuk, Veronica Cartwright, Nancy Cushing-Jones, Dario Dalla Lasta, Donna Dickman, Joan Fontaine, Howard Green, Laurent Hagège, James Hannon, Noelle Hannon, Deborah Hutchison, Hall Hutchison, Cristopher Lapp, Stephan Lapp, Janet Leigh, Kathy Lendeck, Alvin H. Marill, Kirby McCauley, Maitland McDonagh, Jennifer Sebree, Sylvia Sidney, John Springer, and the staff at the Margaret Herrick Library.

Introduction

Why another book on Alfred Hitchcock? Why not? French director François Truffaut wrote in his book *Hitchcock/Truffaut*:

> From the view point of cinema historians, the case of Alfred Hitchcock—both the man and his work—is so rewarding that we can predict that before the end of this century, there will be as many books written about him as there are now about Marcel Proust.

Truffaut was not entirely right; there are today probably more books on Alfred Hitchcock than there are about Marcel Proust or any other writer or director.

Alfred Hitchcock is well known for his innovative visual style. He began his film career during the silent era, which clearly explains why, even in his sound pictures, he relied mostly on his images to convey emotions and thrills. He knew how to establish clever shots and always looked for new ways to tell his stories visually. Hitchcock once said: "One of the worst things a writer can say to me is: 'Well, I'll cover that point in a line of dialogue.' You should stay as visual as you can."

While Hitchcock's visual style has been studied at length, most of the books on the director have not explored the richness of the dialogue in his films. Most of Hitchcock's films were based on novels, plays, and short stories. This is what the director had to say about books in respect to film: "I read the book twice and never look at it again. Then I start from scratch." Hitchcock gave priority to images in his films, but he obviously also knew that a story always had to be told in words before it could be translated to the screen.

Even though he did not write most of his screenplays, Hitchcock worked so closely with his screenwriters that he was able to visualize the film in its entirety before arriving on the set. That process and his fruitful collaboration with writers allowed the director to declare: "When I finally get to work and shoot it, things will be very mundane." Basically, Hitchcock meant that once the shooting began, the screenplay, which he often storyboarded as well, was so detailed that he expected nothing to go wrong and that his job was practically already over!

Just as there are patterns and parallels that can be established in the visual style of Alfred Hitchcock, there is a connection between the characters in his films that becomes more and more obvious if one listens carefully to the dialogue. While Hitchcock's camera flirted, for instance, with the blondes he repeatedly cast in his films, their dialogue expressed their true nature and revealed, more than a camera ever could, how Hitchcock perceived them. Hitchcock said: "I've become a body of films, not a man. I'm all those films." His characters were all part of his universe; they were the expression of his fears, his secret obsessions, his own fantasy world. The words they spoke were Hitchcock's own; his characters were his spokespersons. Therefore, the writing of his films was more essential than it seems, and his collaboration with his screenwriters was probably one of the most important elements in the success of his pictures. On the other hand, his relationship with writers, as much as his collaboration with actors, often required a lot of work. Hitchcock declared:

> One of my biggest problem is writing, and that is why I can't make films more often. No matter how much I try to indoctrinate a writer with my mode of operation, many of them say, "I only see it this way."
>
> Well, they are writers and creative people, but they don't necessarily take the audience into account. I do find that the

bigger the writer, the easier he is to work with. I've had great luck working with men like Ben Hecht, Thornton Wilder, and Robert Sherwood. It's the lesser ones who are the problems. Many of them are writing for their reputation, not for a film. But, of course, I need writers. I am a visual man, but, unfortunately, I also must have delineation of characters and dialogue. The plot I can depict, but I must have convincing characters and dialogue.

Hitchcock was and still is right. Toward the end of his career, he said: "Writers now seem to think it's a sin to have a good story line, but I'm of the opinion that no plot means no film. Most of my films have been rattling good yarns." Movies nowadays are linear and one-dimensional and too often rely on casting and special effects. Characters say what they have to say, and actors deliver their lines without great conviction. Even in Hitchcock's most frightening films, there was humor in the dialogue, and none of the lines were gratuitous. As this book will hopefully prove, the dialogue in Hitchcock's films often had several meanings and could be understood at different levels. This book of quotes is an attempt to establish the missing link between Hitchcock's powerful visuals and the importance of his words.

The first chapter deals with Love, Seduction, and Marriage, followed by chapters on Women, Mothers, Men, Villains and Murder, Food, quotes by Hitchcock and on the master himself by his collaborators or other famous film figures, and finally, quotes from the trailers and ad campaigns for his movies.

Hitchcock directed fifty-six films, but not all of them, especially his early British films, were significant in his career. The quotes chosen for this book are excerpted from Hitchcock's most memorable movies and serve different purposes: They, at times, define the different types of characters Hitchcock liked to deal with in his films. At other times, the quotes are linked more intimately with the director's own personal life. (For example, his obsession with food was present in many of his films, and the dialogue shows that the director associated it with sexuality and in some cases with death and murder.) Other quotes are featured for their pure entertainment value. They are in a way documents of how film dialogue was written in the past and show how subtle and clever it could be—or how heavy-handed and corny—but, of course, always nostalgically charming it was. For the most part, the quotes are presented chronologically, according to the order in which the films were made, unless two quotes were so similar that they needed to be juxtaposed.

Warning: This book is not about the life of Alfred Hitchcock, though I offer some brief biographical data to introduce each theme. Some of the best books on film were written on Alfred Hitchcock. The majority of the quotes by Alfred Hitchcock and about the director are purposely not excerpted from any of these books but from newspaper and magazine clippings in order to complement, not plagiarize, what has already been written in the widely known and read biographies and studies of Alfred Hitchcock. A portion of the quotes from some of Hitchcock's collaborators are also entirely original and exclusive to this book and were selected from interviews I personally conducted.

Ernest Lehman, who wrote *North by Northwest* and *Family Plot* for Hitchcock, once said: "You realize very early when you're working with Hitch, that you're writing for a star, and that star is Alfred Hitchcock." On the other hand, and despite the difficulties of collaborating with a genius such as Hitchcock, the director, as we've already established, acknowledged, to his great distress, the invaluable contribution of his collaborators: "Proper casting not only of performers but of writers," Hitchcock said, "and a close relationship between the artistic and technical people involved in a production are all vitally important to the success of a good suspense film." This book is like a collection of film clips, a guide to the world of Alfred Hitchcock that should reveal, as never before, that as much as his images established that he was a visual genius, his dialogue is the ultimate expression of the secret to his success and to the immortality of his films.

The Alfred Hitchcock Quote Book

Rear Window on Love, Seduction, and Marriage

They met and their life was changed forever...

Alfred Hitchcock created great suspense films, but the fact that he also made great love stories is frequently overlooked. The truth is that love and death were in his work one and the same thing. "In America, you respect him because he shoots scenes of love as if they were scenes of murder," Truffaut declared. "In France, we respect him because he shoots scenes of murder like scenes of love." Often there is more, or as much, intrigue going on between the couples in his films than there is in the actual plot of Hitchcock's greatest thrillers. Obviously, however, before there can be love, a man and a woman must meet.

"I had met her a few years before at the Paramount Studios in London," Hitchcock said of his wife, Alma Reville, "when I was an editorial errand boy told by everybody to keep out of the way. She was already a cutter and producer's assistant and seemed a trifle snooty to me. I couldn't notice Alma without resenting her, and I couldn't help noticing her." Well, this exact situation repeatedly appeared in Hitchcock's films. It's either the man or the woman who seems a trifle snooty; one of the two resents the other, and yet the attraction is always obvious—at least to the audience. In other cases, the man and the woman simply exchange names or a few words, and their life is changed forever.

The 39 Steps

In *The 39 Steps*, RICHARD HANNAY [Robert Donat] is picked up by a mysterious woman named ANNABELLA SMITH [Lucie Mannheim], who turns out to be a spy:

ANNABELLA: May I come home with you?
HANNAY: What's the idea?
ANNABELLA: Well, I'd like to.
HANNAY: Well, it's your funeral.

HANNAY: By the way, am I allowed to know your name?
ANNABELLA: Smith.

Later, at his apartment, Hannay is still seduced but intrigued by his unexpected guest:
HANNAY: I suppose your name isn't really Smith.
ANNABELLA: Depends on where I am. You may call me Annabella.

Secret Agent

RICHARD ASHENDEN [John Gielgud] (*talking to the seductive but rather opinionated* ELSA CARRINGTON [Madeleine Carroll]): Time to tell me who you are, what your name is, and why you're passing yourself off as my wife.

The Lady Vanishes

IRIS HENDERSON [Margaret Lockwood]: You're the most contemptible person I've ever met!
GILBERT REDMAN [Michael Redgrave]: Confidentially, I think you're a bit of a stinker, too.

Rebecca

MAXIM DE WINTER [Laurence Olivier] (*to* SHE* [Joan Fontaine]): Please don't call me Mr. de Winter. I have a very impressive array of first names: George Fortescu Maximilian, but you needn't bother with all of them at once. My family call me Maxim.

Foreign Correspondent

JOHNNY JONES [Joel McCrea]: After all, you don't even know my name yet.
CAROL FISHER [Laraine Day]: Is it necessary?
JOHNNY: Well, it is to me. Don't mind if you hear it's Huntley Haverstock, because it's really Jones. What's yours?
CAROL: Mine is really Smith. Don't mind if you hear it as anything else.

Suspicion

JOHNNY AYSGARTH [Cary Grant] (*to* LINA MCLAIDLAW [Joan Fontaine]): Oh, I beg your pardon. Was that your leg? I had no idea we were going into a tunnel. I thought the compartment was empty.

Spellbound

JOHN BALLANTYNE [Gregory Peck], who suffered from amnesia and recovers his memory: Oh, and by the way, I'm John Ballantyne.
CONSTANCE PETERSEN [Ingrid Bergman]: Oh, I'm very pleased to meet you.

---

*The character played by Joan Fontaine in *Rebecca* does not have a name; in the script she was referred to as "She" or as "the Second Mrs. de Winter."

Stage Fright

WILFRID SMITH [Michael Wilding]: My name is Smith.

EVE GILL [Jane Wyman]: Just ordinary Smith?

WILFRID: Don't call me Mr. Smith. After all, my name is...Wilfrid. Not very good, is it?

EVE: It suits some people very nicely.

Strangers on a Train

BRUNO ANTHONY [Robert Walker] (*to* GUY HAINES [Farley Granger]): I beg your pardon, but aren't you Guy Haines?

To Catch a Thief

In *To Catch a Thief*, FRANCES STEVENS [Grace Kelly] reveals to JOHN ROBIE [Cary Grant] that she knows he is a former jewel thief:

JOHN: I don't know what you're talking about. The police following me?

FRANCES: Yes, police following you, John Robie the Cat!

The Trouble With Harry

SAM MARLOWE [John Forsythe]: What's your given name? If you don't have one to tell me, just make one up.

JENNIFER ROGERS [Shirley MacLaine]: Jennifer. Jennifer Rogers.

Vertigo

In *Vertigo*, MADELEINE ELSTER [Kim Novak] attempts suicide by jumping into the San Francisco Bay and is rescued by JOHN "SCOTTIE" FERGUSON [James Stewart]. Later, they meet more casually (and more seductively) around a fire:

MADELEINE: But I don't know you, and you don't know me. My name is Madeleine Elster.

JOHN: My name is John Ferguson.

MADELEINE: Good strong name. Do your friends call you John or Jack?

JOHN: Oh...John. Mostly old friends call me John. Acquaintances call me Scottie.

MADELEINE: I shall call you Mr. Ferguson.

JOHN: Oh, gee whiz, I wouldn't like that. Oh, no, and after all that happened this afternoon, I would hope you'd call me Scotty, maybe even John.

MADELEINE: Well, I prefer John.

North by Northwest

EVE KENDALL [Eva Marie Saint] introduces herself to ROGER O. THORNHILL [Cary Grant]: I'm Eve Kendall. I'm twenty-six and unmarried. Now you know everything.

ROGER: Jack Philips. Western sales manager for King B. Electronics.

EVE: No, you're not. You're Roger Thornhill of Madison Avenue, and you're wanted for murder on every front page in America, and don't be so modest.

ROGER: Oops!

EVE: Oh, don't worry, I won't say a word.

ROGER: How come?

EVE: I told you...It's a nice face.

EVE: Roger O. Thornhill...What does the "O" stand for?

ROGER: Nothing.

In *North by Northwest*, Hitchcock might have been making fun of producer David O. Selznick, who added the "O" to his name to make it sound more important.

The Birds

MITCH BRENNER [Rod Taylor]: Back in your gilded cage, Melanie Daniels.

MELANIE DANIELS [Tippi Hedren]: What did you say?

MITCH: I was merely drawing a parallel, Miss Daniels.

MELANIE: How do you know my name?

MITCH: A little birdie told me.

Marnie
MARK RUTLAND [Sean Connery]: "Marnie... Yeah, it suits you."

The Art of Seduction

There is another word for seduction: sex. And sex plays an indirect but suggestive and important role in Hitchcock's greatest classics. "My attitude toward sex is the same as it is toward other aspects of my work," Hitchcock once declared, "understatement all the time. I'm not a believer in hanging sex all over a woman. It should be discovered in the course of the story." The scenes of seduction in Hitchcock's films are always extremely sensual, at times humorous, but never distasteful or embarrassing to the audience. Could it be possible that Hitchcock used his films to explore lust and his own carnal appetites? He said: "I've never denied that sex is a vital part of my life. Maybe it's only in my films that my sexual curiosity surfaces, because when it comes to my personal life, I'm certainly not an expert on women." In 1955, to a journalist who was asking him about the many sexual references in his work, he responded: "Concentration on sex? That, my dear lady, is but a regretful look at my own past."

On the set of his film, *The Pleasure Garden*, which he directed in 1925, a young actress refused to do a scene in which she had to swim because she was having her menstrual period. Hitchcock was twenty-five, and his crew had to give the director, whose strict Catholic education did not include such matters, a lesson in female anatomy.

Afterward, Hitchcock was not so innocent, and he left us with films that are an impressive legacy of the art of seduction.

The 39 Steps
PAMELA [Madeleine Carroll]: My shoes and stockings are soaked. I think I'll take them off.

"Can't you realize the only way to clear myself is to expose these spies?"

Robert Donat tries to convince Madeleine Carroll that he is innocent of murder in *The 39 Steps*.

RICHARD HANNAY [Robert Donat]: It's the most sensible thing I've heard you say.

HANNAY is handcuffed to PAMELA and intends to take advantage of the situation.

Young and Innocent
ERICA BURGOYNE [Nova Pilbeam]: Oh, Robert, if only things would turn out all right...
ROBERT TISDALL [Derrick de Marney]: They're starting to.
ERICA: How do you mean?
ROBERT: You called me Robert.
ERICA: Oh, did I? I didn't notice it.

Foreign Correspondent
CAROL FISHER [Laraine Day]: You'd mean much more to me with your clothes on.
JOHNNY JONES [Joel McCrea]: You like the intellectual type.

Suspicion
LINA MCLAIDLAW [Joan Fontaine] (*to* JOHNNY AYSGARTH [Cary Grant]): I don't know how to flirt.

Saboteur
In *Saboteur*, BARRY KANE [Robert Cummings] is wrongly accused of sabotage and tries to seduce PAT MARTIN [Priscilla Lane], a model who won't believe he is innocent:
BARRY: Look, if you'd stop trying to be a hero and decide to be on my side, maybe we could do something about your being cold.
PAT: Build a fire?
BARRY: No. I wasn't exactly thinking of that.

Later, it seems that PAT is really seduced by BARRY:
PAT: Oh, Barry, why couldn't I have met you a hundred years ago on a beach somewhere?
BARRY: Bathing suits looked awfully funny a hundred years ago. I bet you looked beautiful, though.

Stage Fright
In *Stage Fright*, EVE GILL [Jane Wyman] tells WILFRID SMITH [Michael Wilding] that his name is ordinary. From that point on, their conversations become a game of seduction:
EVE: But seriously...Ordinary...Do you think there is something between Cooper and Miss Inwood?
WILFRID: Seriously...Extraordinary...I wouldn't be a bit surprised.

WILFRID: Maybe you're allergic to strange men, too.

EVE: Oh, no, I love strange men...I mean, I'm very fond of them.

Vertigo

In *Vertigo*, JOHN "SCOTTIE" FERGUSON [James Stewart] makes a similar slip with MARGARET ELSTER [Kim Novak] after he saves her from drowning:

MARGARET: The whole thing must have been so embarrassing for you.

JOHN: Not at all, I enjoyed it...Uh...talking to you.

Rear Window

LISA FREEMONT [Grace Kelly] displays her nightgown to her reluctant boyfriend, L.B. JEFFRIES [James Stewart]: Preview of coming attractions.

LISA (*kissing him*): Pay attention to me...

JEFFRIES: I'm not exactly on the other side of the room now.

LISA: Where does a girl have to go before you notice her?

JEFFRIES: Well, if she is pretty enough, she does not have to go anywhere. She just has to be.

LISA: How is your leg.

JEFFRIES: It hurts a little.

LISA: And your stomach?

JEFFRIES: Empty as a football.

LISA: And your love life?

JEFFRIES: Not too active.

LISA: Anything else bothering you?

JEFFRIES: Uh-huh. Who are you?

LISA: Reading from top to bottom, Lisa Carol Freemont.

JEFFRIES: Is this the Lisa Freemont who never wears the same dress twice?

LISA: Only because it's expected of her.

LISA: When I want a man, I want all of him.

The Trouble With Harry
SAM MARLOWE [John Forsythe]: I'd like to paint you nude.
JENNIFER ROGERS [Shirley MacLaine]: Some other time, Mr. Marlowe. I was about to make Arnie some lemonade.

JENNIFER (after SAM kisses her): Lightly, Sam. I have a very short fuse.

Vertigo
MADELEINE ELSTER [Kim Novak]: I'd just thought I'd wonder.
JOHN SCOTTIE FERGUSON [James Stewart]: That's what I was going to do.
MADELEINE: Only one is a wonderer. Two together are always going somewhere.

To Catch a Thief
FRANCES STEVENS [Grace Kelly] suspects that JOHN ROBIE [Cary Grant] is flirting with a French girl:
Are you sure you were talking about water skis? From where I sat, it looked as if you were conjugating some irregular verbs.

FRANCES wants to seduce JOHN:
JOHN: I must say, your terms are generous. Too generous to refuse.
FRANCES: My terms usually are.

JOHN: Miss Stevens, I must say, you are a girl in a million.
FRANCES: That's a routine compliment, but I'll accept it.

JOHN: You're absolutely right. Give me a woman who knows her own mind.

FRANCES: No one gives you a woman like that; you have to capture her.
JOHN: Any particular method?
FRANCES: Yes, but it's no good unless you discover it yourself.

JOHN: Tell me, what do you get a thrill out of most?
FRANCES: I'm still looking for that one.

FRANCES: I've never caught a jewel thief before. It's very stimulating.

FRANCES: You're leaving fingerprints on my arm.

FRANCES: I've the feeling that tonight you're going to see one of the Riviera's most fascinating sights...I was talking about the fireworks.
JOHN: I never doubted that.

FRANCES (*referring to diamonds*): I don't like cold things on my skin.

FRANCES (*referring to her necklace*): Here, hold them... They're the most beautiful thing in the whole world, and the one thing you can't resist.

JOHN: You know as well as I do that this necklace is imitation.
FRANCES: But I'm not...

In both *To Catch a Thief* and *North by Northwest*, Cary Grant is wrongly accused of a crime, and a beautiful blonde wants to protect (read: "seduce") him.

To Catch a Thief
JOHN: May I ask you a personal question?
FRANCES: I've been hoping you would.

JOHN: What do you expect to get out of me by being so nice to me?

FRANCES: Probably a lot more than what you're willing to offer.

JOHN: I know. You're here in Europe to buy a husband.

FRANCES: The man I want does not have a price.

North by Northwest

EVE KENDALL [Eva Marie Saint]: Don't worry, I won't say a word.

ROGER O. THORNHILL [Cary Grant]: How come?

EVE: I told you, it's a nice face.

ROGER: Is that the only reason?

EVE: It's going to be a long night.

ROGER: True.

EVE: And I don't particularly like the book I've started.

ROGER: Ah.

EVE: You know what I mean?

ROGER: Let me think...Yes, I know exactly what you mean...

And later, EVE continues to flirt with ROGER in a train compartment:

ROGER: Tell me, why are you so good to me?

EVE: Shall I climb up and tell you why?

ROGER, (*who has just called for valet service*): Now, what can a man do for twenty minutes with his clothes off? Couldn't we have made it an hour?

EVE: You could take a cold shower.

ROGER (*to* EVE *after kissing her*): Beats flying, doesn't it?

Vertigo

MADELEINE ELSTER [Kim Novak]: I remembered Coit Tower. It led me straight to you.

JOHN "SCOTTIE" FERGUSON [James Stewart]: That's the first time I've been grateful for Coit Tower.

The Birds

In *The Birds*, MITCH BRENNER [Rod Taylor] walks into a bird shop, and MELANIE DANIELS [Tippi Hedren] pretends to be working there to seduce him. He offers no resistance:

MELANIE: There we are. Lovebirds...

MITCH: Those are canaries. Doesn't it make you feel awful?

MELANIE: Doesn't what make me—?

MITCH: To have all these poor, innocent little creatures caged up like this.

MELANIE: Well, we can't just let them fly around the shop, you know.

MITCH: No, I suppose not. Is there an ornithological reason for keeping them in separate cages?

MELANIE: Well, certainly. It's to protect the species.

MITCH: Yes, I suppose that's very important. Especially during the moulting season.

MELANIE: Yes, that's a particularly dangerous time.

MITCH: Are they moulting now?

MELANIE: Some of them are.

MITCH: How can you tell?

MELANIE: Well...they get a sort of hangdog expression.

Family Plot

In *Family Plot*, BLANCHE TYLER [Barbara Harris] is sex starved and constantly trying to seduce her boyfriend, GEORGE LUMLEY [Bruce Dern]. Their dialogue is more than ambiguous.

GEORGE: What's the deal? What do we have to do for the money?

BLANCHE: I'll tell you in bed afterwards.

GEORGE: Come on, Blanche, give me a hint. Just a little foreplay.

BLANCHE: As an actor, you should know fretting will ruin a performance.

GEORGE: You don't have to worry about my performance tonight, honey. As a matter of fact, on this very evening, you're going to get a standing ovation.

GEORGE: Blanche, is that all you've ever got on your mind?

BLANCHE: What are you saving it for? Rainy days?

GEORGE: Honey, you never know when you're going to need it!

GEORGE to BLANCHE: I'm too pooped to pop!

In *Family Plot*, FRAN [Karen Black] needs to seduce her boyfriend, ARTHUR ADAMSON [William Devane], to get some vital piece of information:

FRAN: Where did you put the diamond, dear?

ARTHUR: Where everyone can see it.

FRAN: You didn't!

ARTHUR: I did...

FRAN: Are you gonna tell me where?

ARTHUR: You'll have to torture me first.

FRAN: Oh, I intend to...in a few minutes.

Love Equations

In Hitchcock's work, love and hate often go hand in hand, and these two feelings establish a rather complex, though also thrilling, mysterious, and suspenseful equation. Both love and hate have a direct influence on the plot and play an active role in the resolution of Hitchcock's thrillers. In a good Hitchcock suspense film, the motive force of the story is the love-hate relationship that exists between the characters. To love, one has to hate first; to hate, one has to have loved.

How did Hitchcock deal with love in his own life? Concerning his relationship with his wife, he declared: "Alma is most extraordinary in that she's normal." But Hitchcock also added: "She has a consistency of presence, a never-clouded expression, and she keeps her mouth shut except in magnanimously helpful ways." This remark could easily be perceived as condescending. But in fact, since suspense was everything to Hitchcock, he couldn't have been in love without keeping his feelings at times mysteriously ambiguous; this brought him probably as much satisfaction as when he manipulated his audience.

Rebecca
SHE [Joan Fontaine] (*to* MAXIM DE WINTER [Laurence Olivier]): I don't ask that you should love me. I won't ask the impossible. I'll be your friend, your companion. I'll be happy with that.

MAXIM (*referring to his dead wife*, REBECCA): She was incapable of love or tenderness or decency.

MRS. DANVERS [Judith Anderson] (*referring to* REBECCA): Love was a game to her, only a game.

Foreign Correspondent
JOHNNY JONES [Joel McCrea]: I'm in love with a girl, and I'm going to help hang her father.

Suspicion
LINA MCLAIDLAW [Joan Fontaine]: I couldn't stop loving you if I tried."
JOHNNY AYSGARTH [Cary Grant]: Have you tried?
LINA: Yes.

Lifeboat
In *Lifeboat*, CONSTANCE PORTER [Tallulah Bankhead], a sophisticated and snobbish reporter, falls in love with a rugged, uneducated man named KOVAC [John Hodiak]:

CONSTANCE: That was a dead giveaway, you know, darling, wanting us to die together like that. Dying together is even more personal than living together.

And later, CONSTANCE carries on:
You're a low person, darling. Obviously I forgot it. Maybe that's why I'm attracted to you. Maybe that's why you're attracted to me.

Spellbound

JOHN BALLANTYNE [Gregory Peck] (*describing the symptoms of love*): It was like lightning striking. It strikes rarely.

CONSTANCE PETERSEN [Ingrid Bergman], a psychiatrist, (*as she kisses her patient* JOHN BALLANTYNE *passionately*): I'm here as your doctor only. It has nothing to do with love. Nothing at all. Nothing at all.

JOHN: For what it's worth, I can't remember ever having kissed any other women before.

JOHN: Will you love me just as much when I'm normal?
CONSTANCE: Oh, I'll be insane about you!

CONSTANCE (*referring to the fact that* JOHN BALLANTYNE *is suspected of murder*): I couldn't feel this way toward a man who was bad, who had committed murder. I couldn't feel this pain for someone who was evil.

DR. ALEX BRULOV [Michael Chekhov] explains to CONSTANCE, his friend and former student, his theory on women and love:
Women make the best psychoanalysts until they fall in love. After that, they make the best patients.
And later:
We both know that the mind of a woman in love is operating on the lowest level of the intellect.

Notorious

In *Notorious*, DEVLIN [Cary Grant] won't admit that he is in love with ALICIA HUBERMAN [Ingrid Bergman], a disillusioned woman, until her life is in danger:

ALICIA: There is nothing like a love song to give you a good laugh!

ALICIA: You're scared of yourself. You're afraid you'll fall in love with me.

ALICIA: This is a very strange love affair.
DEVLIN: Why?
ALICIA: Maybe the fact that you don't love me.
DEVLIN: When I don't love you, I'll let you know.

ALICIA: Don't ever leave me.
DEVLIN: You'll never get rid of me again.
ALICIA: I never tried to.

ALEXANDER SEBASTIAN [Claude Rains] (*to* ALICIA): It's not that I don't trust you. When you're in love at my age, any man who looks at you is a menace.

The Paradine Case

Love makes the characters in *The Paradine Case* feel rather insecure about themselves:

GAY KEANE [Ann Todd] (*to her husband,* ANTHONY [Gregory Peck]): I may not be the cleverest woman in the world, and there's lots of things I don't know. But there is one thing I know better than anyone. I know you.

LADY HORFIELD [Ethel Barrymore] (*to her husband,* LORD HORFIELD [Charles Laughton]): I might be silly, Tommy, but I love you. I've always loved you.

ANTHONY KEANE (*to his client* MRS. PARADINE [Valli]): And I was idiot enough to fall in love with you.

MRS. PARADINE (*to her lawyer,* ANTHONY KEANE): You're my lawyer, not my lover.

MRS. PARADINE (*referring to her valet,* ANDRE LATOUR [Louis Jourdan], *whom she loves and wants to protect*): You are not to destroy him. If you do, I shall hate you like I've never hated a man.

GAY KEANE (*referring to her husband*): I don't own him, I only love him.

I Confess
RUTH GRANDFORT [Anne Baxter] (*to her lover,* FATHER MICHAEL LOGAN [Montgomery Clift]): Are you afraid of me? Why? Why? You're in love with me. You've always been in love with me. You haven't changed.

Dial M for Murder
TONY WENDICE [Ray Milland] (*referring to his wife* [Grace Kelly] *and her lover* [Robert Cummings]): It's funny how you can tell when people are in love...

Rear Window
In *Rear Window,* LISA FREEMONT [Grace Kelly] and L. B. JEFFRIES [James Stewart] have a lover's quarrel:
JEFFRIES: When am I going to see you again?
LISA: Not for a while. At least not until tomorrow.

LISA (*referring to a love song*): It's almost as if it were being written especially for us.
JEFFRIES (*referring to the struggling songwriter who composed it*): No wonder he is having so much trouble with it.

Vertigo
In *Vertigo,* JOHN "SCOTTIE" FERGUSON [James Stewart] falls in love with MADELEINE ELSTER [Kim Novak], who pretends to

be a disturbed woman and whose real name is JUDY BARTON:
JOHN: I'm here. I got you.
MADELEINE: Don't leave me. Stay with me.
JOHN: All the time.

JOHN (*to* MADELEINE): I'm responsible for you now. You know, the Chinese say that once you've saved a person's life, you're responsible for it forever. So, I'm committed.

MADELEINE: You believe I love you.
JOHN: Yes.
MADELEINE: Then if you lose me, you'll know I loved you and I wanted to go on loving you.
JOHN: I won't lose you.
MADELEINE: Let me go into the church.

JOHN: We could see a lot of each other.
JUDY: Why? Because I remind you of her? It's not very complimentary. Anything else?
JOHN: No.
JUDY: It's not very complimentary, either.

JUDY: I made the mistake. I fell in love. It wasn't part of the plan.

So that JOHN will love her, JUDY is ready to impersonate MADELEINE:
If I let you change it, would that do it? If I do what you tell me, will you love me?

North by Northwest
EVE KENDALL [Eva Marie Saint]: You make women who don't know you fall in love with you.
ROGER O. THORNHILL [Cary Grant]: I'm beginning to think I'm underpaid.

The Birds

In *The Birds*, MELANIE DANIELS [Tippi Hedren] arrives in Bodega Bay under the false pretense of bringing lovebirds to MITCH BRENNER's [Rod Taylor] sister. But she does not fool ANNIE HAYWORTH [Suzanne Pleshette], Mitch's former girlfriend:

ANNIE: Pretty. What are they?

MELANIE: Lovebirds.

ANNIE: Mmmm...Well, good luck, Miss Daniels.

And she doesn't fool Mitch's mother, LYDIA [Jessica Tandy], either:

LYDIA: You did say birds.

MITCH: Lovebirds.

LYDIA: I see.

ANNIE: I wanted to be near Mitch. It was over, and I knew it, but I wanted to be near him, anyway. You see, I still like him a lot. That's rare, I think. I don't want to lose his friendship...ever.

Marnie

MARK RUTLAND [Sean Connery] (*to* MARNIE [Tippi Hedren]): Well, it seems to be my misfortune to have fallen in love with a thief and a liar.

The Words We All Want to Hear

"The day I proposed marriage to Alma she was lying in an upper bunk of a ship's cabin," Hitchcock recalled. "The ship was flondering in a most desperate way, and so was Alma, who was sick...As it was, she groaned, nodded her head, and burped. It was one of my greatest scenes—a little weak on dialogue, perhaps, but beautifully staged and not overplayed."

Love declarations and marriage proposals become pivotal moments in the films of Alfred Hitchcock. They constitute yet another twist that not only changes the destiny of the characters but also complicates the plot. When asked what was the most important thing in his life, François Truffaut replied without any hesitation, "Movies!" Hitchcock was more generous and once said: "I had wanted to become, first, a movie director and, second, Alma's husband." It seems he certainly realized his ambitions. In his films, things were more unpredictable, especially when it came to love declarations and marriage proposals.

Love Declarations

Sabotage

TED SPENSER [John Loder], a detective, declares his love to MRS. VERLOC [Sylvia Sidney] before he plans to arrest her husband and finds out she killed him: I know this isn't a very good time to tell you. I shouldn't tell you at all, I suppose. But before I take him along, I want you to know that what happens to you means a lot to me. I didn't want to tell you how I felt about you, but there it is.

Secret Agent

ELSA CARRINGTON [Madeleine Carroll] (to RICHARD ASHENDEN [John Gielgud]): I fell in love with you at first sight.

Foreign Correspondent

JOHNNY JONES [Joel McCrea] (to CAROL FISHER [Laraine Day]): If you knew how much I love you, you'd faint.

JOHNNY, who has fallen in love with CAROL FISHER, the daughter of a spy: Listen, I'm in love with you. I can't hit you over the head with a scandal for a wedding present!

Sylvia Sidney and John Loder in *Sabotage*.

"I remember watching the film and being shocked by the fact that I played a woman who murders her husband and who walks out into the night with a lover who happens to be a detective! I have no idea how Hitchcock got away with this because I found the plot immoral. I think she should have paid for her crime." —Sylvia Sidney.

Suspicion
LINA MCLAIDLAW [Joan Fontaine] (*to* ANTHONY AYSGARTH [Cary Grant]): I hope I'm not saying the wrong thing, but I think I love you.

Shadow of a Doubt
In *Shadow of a Doubt*, JACK GRAHAM [Macdonald Carey], an undercover detective, declares his love to CHARLIE NEWTON [Teresa Wright]: I like it when you laugh. I like it when you don't. I guess I like you whatever you do. I guess I like you.

I can't help it, I want to tell you now. I love you, Charlie. I love you terribly.

Listen, Charlie, when I go away, will you go back to that square in the middle of the town and take a good look at it—because that's where I first knew I loved you.

Spellbound
CONSTANCE PETERSEN [Ingrid Bergman] (*to* JOHN BALLANTYNE [Gregory Peck]): You said you loved me. Look at me. Why am I fighting for you? Because I love you.

Notorious
ALICIA HUBERMAN [Ingrid Bergman]: You love me. Why didn't you tell me before?
DEVLIN [Cary Grant]: I know. But I could not see straight or think straight. I was a fat-headed guy full of pain. It tore me up not having you.
ALICIA: You love me. You love me.
DEVLIN: Long ago. All the time. Since the beginning.

ALICIA: Say it again. It keeps me awake.
DEVLIN: I love you.

Stage Fright

EVE GILL [Jane Wyman] (*to* WILFRID SMITH [Michael Wilding]): When we were in the taxi together, I felt as though I was on a great golden cloud.

Rear Window

LISA FREEMONT [Grace Kelly] (*to* L. B. JEFFRIES [James Stewart], *a reporter*): I'm in love with you. I don't care what you do for a living. I'd just like to be part of it somehow.

I Confess

RUTH GRANDFORT [Anne Baxter] (*to* FATHER MICHAEL LOGAN [Montgomery Clift]): I love you, Michael. I've always been in love with you. I know, I know it's wrong. I can't help it.

To Catch a Thief

FRANCES STEVENS [Grace Kelly]: I'm in love with you.

JOHN ROBIE [Cary Grant]: That's a ridiculous thing to say.

Marnie

MARK RUTLAND [Sean Connery]: Whatever you are, I love you. It's horrible, I know, but I do love you.

MARNIE EDGAR [Tippi Hedren]: You don't love me. I'm just something you caught. You think I'm some kind of animal you've trapped.

MARK: That's right, you are, and I caught something really wild this time, haven't I? I've tracked you and caught you, and by God I'm going to keep you.

Marriage Proposals

Rebecca

MAXIM DE WINTER [Laurence Olivier]: Either you go to America with Mrs. Van Hopper or you come home to Manderley with me.

SHE [Joan Fontaine]: You mean you want a secretary or something?

MAXIM: I'm asking you to marry me, you little fool.

Foreign Correspondent

CAROL [Laraine Day]: You're just a wee bit unscrupulous, aren't you?

JOHNNY [Joel McCrea]: Not unscrupulous, just in love. The same thing, I suppose.

CAROL: I beg your pardon...

JOHNNY: I beg yours. You see, I love you, and I want to marry you.

CAROL: I love you, and I want to marry you.

JOHNNY: That narrows things down quite a bit, doesn't it?

CAROL: Do you mind?

JOHNNY: Not at all. It's made a new man out of me.

CAROL: Well, I hope not entirely new. It took me quite some time to get used to the first man you were.

JOHNNY: To be perfectly frank with you, I expected a little more argument. Now I'm really left with quite a few things I wanted very much to say.

CAROL: Save them until we're married. I imagine they'll sound much better then.

Suspicion

JOHNNY AYSGARTH [Cary Grant] (*talking to the portrait of his future wife's father*): Sir, I have the honor of asking for your daughter's hand in marriage.

Shadow of a Doubt

JACK GRAHAM [Macdonald Carey], a detective (*to* CHARLIE NEWTON) [Teresa Wright]): I suppose it couldn't ever really happen someday that you'd tell your father about marrying someone. A detective, I mean...

Spellbound

JOHN BALLANTYNE [Gregory Peck]: You'll look wonderful in white with a little orange blossom in your hair.

CONSTANCE PETERSEN [Ingrid Bergman]: This sounds vaguely like something to do with marriage.

JOHN: That's a brilliant analysis, Doctor.

The Trouble With Harry

JENNIFER ROGERS [Shirley MacLaine]: I've decided, Sam.

SAM MARLOWE [John Forsythe]: Decided what?

JENNIFER: I will marry you if you haven't forgotten about asking me. I'm very fond of you, and I think you'd make a good father for Arnie and for some other reasons better left unsaid.

North by Northwest

ROGER O. THORNHILL [Cary Grant]: If we ever get out of this alive, let's go back to New York on the train together, all right?

EVE KENDALL [Eva Marie Saint]: Is that a proposition?

ROGER: It's a proposal, sweetie.

Marnie

MARNIE EDGAR [Tippi Hedren]: What are you trying to pull?

MARK RUTLAND [Sean Connery]: I'm trying to pull a proposal. Let's see, how should I phrase it? How about, will you be mine?

Marriage Is Hell

Alfred Hitchcock received the Life Achievement Award from the American Film Institute in 1978 and declared to the audience:

Four people have given me the most affection, appreciation and encouragement, and constant collaboration. The first of the four is a film editor. The second is a scriptwriter, the third is the mother of my daughter, Pat, and the fourth is the finest cook who has ever performed miracles in a domestic kitchen. Their names are Alma Reville.

Alma not only was Hitchcock's faithful wife, but as the director pointed out to people who accused him of overshadowing her, she did most of his script reading, worked closely on the entire production of his films, and Hitchcock relied completely on her opinion when it came to the decisions he had to make in his work. In appearance, Hitchcock and his wife were happy together, though many books on the director's life have speculated on whether the couple only had a strong partnership instead of a, let's say, conventional marriage. One thing is certain however: In his films, marriage was never, except in a few rare occasions, a perfect ordeal and was often directly linked to death or at least referred to as a depressing element of life.

The Lodger (title card)
JOE BETTS [Malcolm Keen]: When I've put a rope round the Avenger's neck, I'll put a ring round Daisy's finger.

The Man Who Knew Too Much* (1934)
JILL LAWRENCE [Edna Best] (to her husband BOB [Leslie Banks]): I'm just going off with another man. Darling, you go to bed early with Betty.

The 39 Steps
In *The 39 Steps*, RICHARD HANNAY [Robert Donat] is pursued by dangerous killers. He asks the MILKMAN* to help him:
HANNAY: It's quite true. Listen. They're spies. Foreigners. They've murdered a woman in my flat, and now they're after me.

---

*The first of Hitchcock's two versions of this film.
*Several names of actors are unavailable.

MILKMAN: Oh, come off it. Funny jokes at five o'clock in the morning...

HANNAY: All right, all right. I'll tell you the truth. Are you married?

MILKMAN: Yes, but don't rub it in. What's the idea now?

HANNAY: Well, I'm not—You see, I'm a bachelor.

MILKMAN: Are you?

HANNAY: A married woman lives on the first floor.

MILKMAN: Does she?

HANNAY: Yes, and I've been paying her a call, and I want to go home.

MILKMAN: Well, what's preventing you?

HANNAY: One of these men happen to be her husband.

MILKMAN: Why didn't you tell me before, old fellow?

After he's loaned his outfit to Hannay, the milkman concludes:
You'll do the same thing for me one day.

A MAN's [Gus McNaughton] comment about a rather unsexy woman's corset: Brrr! My wife!

HANNAY (*referring to a lovely young woman played by Peggy Ashcroft*): Your daughter?

THE CROFTER [John Laurie]: My wife.

Secret Agent

In *Secret Agent*, RICHARD ASHENDEN [John Gielgud] and ELSA CARRINGTON [Madeleine Carroll] are two spies who have to pretend they're married even though they've never met before:

RICHARD: What do you think of your new husband?

ELSA: I'm agreeably surprised.

ELSA (after RICHARD slaps her): Married life has begun.

ELSA: What do you think of me?

RICHARD: Don't know. I'll tell you when you've finished putting on your face.

Marnie
MARK RUTLAND [Sean Connery] (*to his disturbed wife,* MARNIE [Tippi Hedren]): You look very sexy with your face clean.

Young and Innocent
GUY [George Curzon] (*to his wife,* CHRISTINE [Pamela Carme], *before he murders her*): You're a liar. A liar. You lied to me when you married me. You lied to get rid of me. You're a liar and a cheat.

The Lady Vanishes
In *The Lady Vanishes*, IRIS HENDERSON [Margaret Lockwood] is on her way to get married because it is expected of her. Even her friends know that she is making a terrible mistake:

JULIE [Sally Stewart]: To Iris and the happy days she's leaving behind!

IRIS: I've no regrets. I've been everywhere and done everything. I've eaten caviar at Cannes, sausage rolls at the dogs. I've played baccarat at Biarritz and darts with the rural dean. What is there left for me but marriage?

JULIE: Well, there's still time to change your mind, Iris.
BLANCHE [Googie Withers]: Yes, why not send Charles a greeting telegram and tell him he's all washed up?
IRIS: No, it's too late. This time next week, I shall be a slightly sunburnt offering on an altar in Hanover Square. I shan't mind really.

IRIS meets GILBERT REDMAN [Michael Redgrave], an obnoxious musician. They hate each other at first and then, logically, fall in love:

GILBERT: You dare to call it noise! The ancient music with which your present ancestors celebrated every wedding for countless generations! The dance they danced when your father married your mother, always supposing you were born in wedlock, which I doubt.

GILBERT: My father always taught me, never desert a lady in trouble. He even carried that as far as marrying mother.

IRIS: I'm being married on Thursday.
GILBERT: You're quite sure you're not imagining that?
IRIS: Positive.
GILBERT: I was afraid so.

MARGARET [Linden Travers], a woman who is traveling with her lover: If there's a scandal, there'll be a divorce. You couldn't let me down, could you? You'd have to do the decent thing as reluctantly as only you know how.
MR. TODHUNTER [Cecil Parker]: You forget one thing, Margaret. Your husband would divorce you, I've no doubt, but whatever happens, my wife will never divorce me.

Jamaica Inn
MARY [Maureen O'Hara]: This is your last chance to be free of him, your last chance!
PATIENCE [Marie Ney]: No!
MARY: But he is a wrecker, a murderer!
PATIENCE: But he is my husband...

Rebecca
MAXIM DE WINTER [Laurence Olivier] (*to* SHE [Joan Fontaine] *after she accepts his marriage proposal*): Now, that's settled. You may pour me out some coffee. Two ounces of sugar and some milk. Same with my tea, don't forget.

SHE: I suppose that's why you married me, because you knew

Alfred Hitchcock, Joan Fontaine, and Laurence Olivier on the set of *Rebecca*.

"He had great respect for women. He was very close to his wife and adored her and his daughter, Patricia. He was easy going, almost placid. The only time he ever raised his voice was to say something humorous." —Joan Fontaine.

I was dull and gauche and inexperienced and that there had never been any gossip about me.

MAXIM: I wonder if I did a very selfish thing in marrying you. And later:
You ought to have married a boy.

MAXIM (*referring to his deceased wife*, REBECCA): She's got the three things that really mattered in a wife, everyone said: breeding, brains, and beauty, and I believed them completely. But I never had a moment of happiness with her.

MAXIM (*referring to his pathetic marriage to* REBECCA): She knew that I'd sacrifice anything than stand up in a divorce court and give her away, admit that our marriage was a rotten fraud.

Mr. and Mrs. Smith

ANN [Carole Lombard] and DAVID SMITH [Robert Montgomery] have a rather compromised marriage in *Mr. and Mrs. Smith*:
ANN: Respect for each other as individuals, that's what counts. Always tell the truth no matter what the consequences. You see, I think if we told each other just one lie, we would have to admit we failed, wouldn't we?
DAVID: Uh-huh.
ANN: And what would we have left? Marriage like other people.

ANN: A wife should conduct herself to please her husband.

ANN: If you had it all to do over again, would you've married me?
DAVID: Honestly, no. Not that I want to be married to anyone else, but I think that when a man gets married, he gives up a certain amount of freedom and independence. If I had to do it all over again, I think I would stay single.

DAVID: Darling, I do want to be married to you. I love you, I worship you, I am used to you.

ANN (*to* JEFF [Gene Raymond], *her husband's business partner*): What a beautiful room! No wonder you've never gotten married!

ANN: I'm not innocent.
DAVID: There you are. She admits she is my wife!

Suspicion

COLONEL MCLAIDLAW [Sir Cedric Hardwicke] (*referring to his daughter*, LINA [Joan Fontaine]): Lina will never marry. She is not the marrying sort.

JOHNNY AYSGARTH [Cary Grant]: Lina?
LINA: Yes, dear.
JOHNNY: Do you ever have any regrets that you married me?
LINA: Why do you ask that?
JOHNNY: Well, it seems pretty obvious that your father would have left you a lot more than his portrait if you had been anybody else but Mrs. John Aysgarth.

Saboteur

In *Saboteur*, BARRY KANE [Robert Cummings] travels with a TRUCK DRIVER [Murray Alper], who has a rather unhappy marriage:
TRUCK DRIVER: Are you married?
BARRY: No.
TRUCK DRIVER: Go ahead and whistle!

Later, the TRUCK DRIVER carries on:
I never see anything happen. I don't ever hear about anything except when my wife tells me what she sees in the moving pictures. That's the way she spends the money, moving pictures and new hats. Buys a new hat so that she can put it on to go to the picture show so that she can take it off.

Shadow of a Doubt

ANN NEWTON [Edna May Wonacott], a young and precocious girl: Sing at the table, you'll marry a crazy husband.

MRS. POTTER*: There is one good thing in being a widow, isn't there? You don't have to ask your husband for money.

---

*Several names of actors are unavailable.

ANN (*referring to her mother*): She thinks girls ought to marry and settle down.

EMMA NEWTON [Patricia Collinge] (*referring to her brother,* CHARLIE [Joseph Cotten]): But you see, we were so close growing up. And then Charles ran away, I got married, and...then, you know how it is. You sort of forget you're you. Then you're your husband's wife.

Notorious
ALEXANDER SEBASTIAN [Claude Rains]: I'm married to an American agent.

Spellbound
DETECTIVE (*to* CONSTANCE PETERSEN [Ingrid Bergman]): I'm a married man myself, and I know how it feels like to have a wife come chasing after you to apologize.

DR. ALEX BRULOV [Michael Chekhov] (*to* JOHN BALLANTYNE [Gregory Peck]): Any husband of Constance is a husband of mine, so to speak.

The Paradine Case
ANTHONY KEANE [Gregory Peck] to his wife, GAY [Ann Todd]): Really, darling, there are more important things than anniversaries.

LADY HORFIELD [Ethel Barrymore]: Your husband is very clever, isn't he?
GUY KEANE: Yes, I think so.
LADY HORFIELD: So is mine. I'm not sure that I like it.

JUDY FLAQUER [Joan Tetzel]: The best men always end up with the worst women.

Stage Fright

CHARLOTTE INWOOD [Marlene Dietrich] (*referring to her late husband*): He was an abominable man. Why do women marry abominable men?

MRS. GILL [Dame Sybil Thorndike] (*introducing her husband* [Alastair Sim]): Mr. Smith, this is Eve's father. We see him now and again.

COMMODORE GILL [Alastair Sim]: Forgiveness, Mr. Smith, the secret of a happy married life. That and good long stretches of absence that make the heart grow fonder.

Strangers on a Train

BRUNO ANTHONY [Robert Walker]: When is the wedding?
GUY HAINES [Farley Granger]: What?
BRUNO: The wedding... You and Ann Morton. It was in the papers.
GUY: It shouldn't have been unless they legalized bigamy overnight.
BRUNO: Oh, I've a wonderful theory about that.

GUY (*to his wife*, MIRIAM HAINES [Laura Elliot]): It's pretty late to start flirting with a discarded husband, especially when you're having another man's baby.

Dial M for Murder

TONY WENDICE [Ray Milland] (*referring to his wife*, MARGOT [Grace Kelly]): She tried to make me give up tennis and play husband instead.

TONY: You can always marry for money.
LESGATE [Anthony Dawson]: Yes, I suppose some people make a business out of that.
TONY: I know I did.

Vertigo
JOHN "SCOTTIE" FERGUSON [James Stewart]: How did you get in the ship building, Gavin?
GAVIN ELSTER [Tom Helmore]: I married it.

Rear Window
In *Rear Window*, L. B. JEFFRIES [James Stewart] is against marriage despite the efforts of LISA FREEMONT [Grace Kelly] to seduce him and the efforts of his nurse, STELLA [Thelma Ritter], and his editor, GUNESON [only a voice on the phone], to convince him otherwise:

JEFFRIES: If you don't pull me out of this swamp of boredom, I'm going to do something drastic. Like what? ... Like getting married; then I'll never be able to go anywhere.
GUNESON (on the phone): It's about time you got married before you turn into a lonesome and bitter old man.
JEFFRIES: Can't you just see me rushing home to a hot apartment to listen to the automatic laundry and the electric dishwasher and the garbage disposal and a nagging old wife.
GUNESON: Jeff, wives just don't nag anymore, they discuss.
JEFFRIES: Is that so? Maybe in a high-rent district they discuss; in my neighborhood, they still nag.
GUNESON: Yeah? You know best.

STELLA: Every man is ready for marriage when the right girl comes along, and Lisa Freemont is the right girl for any man with half a brain who can get one eye open.

JEFFRIES (*referring to* LISA): She expects me to marry her.
STELLA: That's normal.
JEFFRIES: I don't want to.
STELLA: That's abnormal.

STELLA: Some of the world's happiest marriages have started under the guns, as you might say.

STELLA: Look, Mr. Jeffries, I'm not an educated woman, but I can tell you one thing: When a man and a woman see each other and like each other, they ought to come together, wham! like a couple of taxis on Broadway... Not sit around analyzing each other like two specimens in a bottle.

STELLA: Intelligence. Nothing has caused the human race so much trouble as intelligence. Ah! Modern marriage!

JEFFRIES: We've progressed emotionally.

STELLA: Baloney! Once, it was see somebody, get excited, get married. Now it's read a lot of books, fence with a lot of four-syllable words, psychoanalyze each other until you can't tell the difference between a petting party and a civil service exam.

STELLA: When I married Miles, we were both a couple of maladjusted misfits. We are still maladjusted misfits, and we've loved every minute of it.

STELLA: You ever gonna get married?

JEFFRIES: I'll probably get married one of these days, and when I do, it's gonna be to someone who thinks of life not just as a new dress, a lobster dinner, the latest scandal.

JEFFRIES: There is an intelligent way to approach marriage.

STELLA: Lisa is loaded to her fingertips with love for you. I've got two words of advice for you: Marry her!

JEFFRIES (*referring to one of his neighbors*): He lives alone. Probably had a very unhappy marriage.

LISA (*referring to another one of* JEFFRIES's *lonely neighbors*): Maybe one day she'll find happiness.

JEFFRIES: And a man will lose his.

A WIFE: If you had told me you had quit your job, we wouldn't have gotten married.
HER HUSBAND: Oh, honey, come on.

To Catch a Thief

FRANCES STEVENS [Grace Kelly]: You never mentioned your wife.
JOHN ROBIE [Cary Grant]: Never found the time to get married.

The Trouble With Harry

In *The Trouble With Harry*, SAM MARLOWE [John Forsythe] wants to marry JENNIFER ROGERS [Shirley MacLaine], whose husband was just found dead:
SAM (*referring to* JENNIFER's *dead husband*): What did he do to you besides marry you?

JENNIFER: You want to marry me?
SAM: Uh-huh. Why not?
JENNIFER: Because I just got my freedom today.
SAM: Easy come, easy go...Besides, if you marry me, you'll keep your freedom.
JENNIFER: You must be practically unique, then.
SAM: I respect freedom. More than that, I love freedom. We might be the only free married couple in the world.

JENNIFER (*referring to* HARRY, *her dead husband*): Frankly, I don't care what you do with Harry just as long as you don't bring him back to life.

SAM: Harry...We're not quite finished with him yet.
JENNIFER: Well, Sam, if anybody is through with Harry, he's been buried three times.
SAM: Before we get married, you're going to have to prove that

you're free. To prove that you're free, you'll have to prove that Harry is...

JENNIFER: ...Dead. What a horrible complication.

The Man Who Knew Too Much (1956)

MRS. DRAYTON [Brenda De Banzie] (*complaining about her husband* [Bernard Miles] *to* JO MCKENNA [Doris Day], *a former singer*): Of course, we hardly ever see a show now. Edward is such a stick in the mud, so I have to console myself with your records.

BEN MCKENNA [James Stewart] and his wife, JO, have a difficult but solid marriage:

BEN: It's just that I'm a doctor, and you know a doctor's wife never has as much time to do—

JO: What my husband is trying to say is that the Broadway shows aren't produced in Indianapolis, Indiana. Of course, we could live in New York. I hear that doctors aren't starving there, either.

BEN: After all, you can't blame him for turning down an old married couple like us for a girl like that.

JO: We're not an old married couple!

JO: Darling, I'm not the police inspector. I'm your wife!

The Wrong Man

In *The Wrong Man*, ROSE BALESTRERO [Vera Miles] feels responsible for the bad luck that has befallen her husband [Henry Fonda]:

The truth is I've let you down, Manny. I haven't been a good wife.

Vertigo

In *Vertigo*, MIDGE WOOD [Barbara Bel Geddes] is secretly in love with JOHN "SCOTTIE" FERGUSON [James Stewart]:

JOHN: How is your love life, Midge?
MIDGE: It's following a train of thought.
JOHN: Well?
MIDGE: Normal.
JOHN: Aren't you ever gonna get married?
MIDGE: You know there is only one man in the world for me, Johnny-O.
JOHN: You mean me. We were engaged once, weren't we?
MIDGE: Three whole weeks.
JOHN: Good old college days. But you were the one who called off the engagement, remember? I'm still available. Available Ferguson.

MADELEINE ELSTER [Kim Novak]: One shouldn't live alone.
JOHN: Some people prefer it.
MADELEINE: No, it's wrong. I'm married, you know.

North by Northwest
ROGER O. THORNHILL [Cary Grant] (*to the doorman of his office building*): Good night, Eddie. Say hello to the Mrs.
EDDIE: We're not talking.

ROGER: What's wrong with men like me?
EVE KENDALL [Eva Marie Saint]: They don't believe in marriage.
ROGER: I've been married twice.
EVE: See what I mean.

EVE and ROGER's conversation about marriage continues as they're being chased by two killers on top of Mount Rushmore:
EVE: What happened to your first two marriages?
ROGER: My wives divorced me.
EVE: Why?
ROGER: I think they thought I led too dull a life!

Psycho

In *Psycho*, MARION CRANE [Janet Leigh] is tired of meeting her lover, SAM LOOMIS [John Gavin], in cheap hotel rooms at lunchtime. She wants to marry him, while he is still trying to recover from a divorce:

SAM: I've heard of married couples who deliberately spend an occasional night in a cheap hotel. They say it's very exciting.

MARION: Oh, when you're married, you can do a lot of exciting things deliberately.

SAM: You sure talk like a girl who's been married.

Later, the argument continues:

SAM: A couple of years and the debts will be paid off, and if she ever remarries, the alimony stops and—

MARION: I haven't been married once yet!

SAM: Yeah, but when you do, you'll swing!

But MARION insists:

MARION: Sam, let's get married!

SAM: Yeah! And live with me in a storeroom behind a hardware store in Fairvale? We'll have lots of laughs! I tell you what. When I send my ex-wife alimony, you can lick the stamps!

MARION: I'll lick the stamps.

SAM: Marion, you want to cut this off—go out and find yourself somebody available?

MARION: I'm thinking of it.

SAM: How could you even think a thing like that?

MARION steals money from an obnoxious man named CASSIDY [Frank Albertson], who has his own views on marriage:

CASSIDY: I'm buying this house for my baby's wedding present. Forty thousand dollars. Cash! Now that's not buying happiness. That's just buying off unhappiness.

CAROLINE [Patricia Hitchcock], who works with Marion, is jealous of CASSIDY's flirting with her colleague: He was flirting with you. I guess he must have noticed my wedding ring.

SHERIFF CHAMBERS [John McIntire]: Mrs. Bates poisoned this guy she was involved with when she found out he was married.

The Birds

MITCH BRENNER [Rod Taylor] is a lawyer. MELANIE DANIELS [Tippi Hedren] is referring here to one of his clients: Why did he shoot her?
MITCH: He was watching a ball game on television.
MELANIE: What?
MITCH: His wife changed the channel.

LYDIA BRENNER [Jessica Tandy] to MELANIE: I lost my husband four years ago, you know. It's terrible how you depend on someone else for strength and suddenly all the strength is gone and you're alone.

Marnie

MARNIE EDGAR [Tippi Hedren]: I didn't want to get married. It's degrading. It's animal.

MARNIE free-associates with her husband, MARK RUTLAND [Sean Connery]: Now, you give me a word, and I give you an association. You know, like needles, pins, when a man gets married, trouble begins.

MARK: This is the drill, dear. Wife follows husband to the front door, gives and/or gets a kiss. Stands pensively as he drives away. Oh, a wistful little wave is optional.

Torn Curtain

SARAH SHERMAN [Julie Andrews] (in bed, kissing her fiancé, MICHAEL ARMSTRONG [Paul Newman]): Now listen, dear, what is your position on a June wedding?

Topaz

ANDRE DEVEREAUX [Frederick Stafford]: Diplomats' wives should not talk!
NICOLE, his wife [Dany Robin]: All wives talk.

JACQUES GRANVILLE [Michel Piccoli] (*to his mistress, a married woman*): Thanks for coming.
NICOLE: Why shouldn't I come? I'm a free woman.

Frenzy

In *Frenzy*, RICHARD BLANEY [Jon Finch], has divorced his wife, BRENDA [Barbara Leigh-Hunt], who since then has opened a successful matrimonial agency:
MRS. DAVISON [Madge Ryan], one of her clients leaves her office with a new husband [George Tovey]: Did you know that my late husband, Mr. Davison, was up at five-thirty every morning of his life and by the time he brought me my cup of tea, which he did punctually at nine-fifteen, he would have cleaned the whole house. He was so quiet about it that he never woke me once. Not once.

RICHARD is not especially enthusiastic about his ex-wife's new career: You can inform Mrs. Blaney that one of her less successful exercises in matrimony has come to see her.

I'm amazed that in an age where practically everybody considers marriage is hell that you can find clients.

I bet you're making a fortune out of that agency. And why not? If you can't make love, sell it! The respectable kind, of course, the married kind.

Family Plot

GEORGE LUMLEY [Bruce Dern]: Now Blanche, have you got any idea what you and I could do with ten grand?

BLANCHE TYLER [Barbara Harris]: Uh-huh. We could even get married.
GEORGE: What are you always a wet blanket for?
BLANCHE: Don't you flatter me so.

But marriage can also be positive...

Suspicion
JOHNNY AYSGARTH [Cary Grant] (*to* LINA MCLAIDLAW [Joan Fontaine]): Monkey face, marrying you is the one thing I'll never change my mind about.
    And later:
Marrying you is the sanest thing I've ever done.

Rope
RUPERT CADELL [James Stewart] (*referring to the cook* [Edith Evanson]): Wonderful Mrs. Wilson. I might marry her.

The Trouble With Harry
CAPT. ALBERT WILES [Edmund Gwenn]: Marriage is a good way to spend the winter.

Ladies Don't Vanish

What did Hitchcock say about women?

"I find women very difficult creatures. Very difficult indeed. I don't know why, but I've never been able to figure them out. It seems so often they just go off the deep end. Pffffft! Just like that, without any logical explanation whatsoever."

"Not being a woman, I don't know what femininity is."

"The typical American woman is a tease—dresses for sex and doesn't give it. A man puts his hand on her, and she runs screaming for mother. English women are the opposite—outwardly cool, but, boy, underneath!"

"I think the English women are the worst. You know, they all look like schoolteachers, but in a taxi cab, they'll tear you to pieces."

"I've never wanted to have the obvious blonde, the one who has her sex hanging around her neck like jewelry, the big-bosomed girl. Neither the Marilyn Monroe nor the Jean Harlow type was for me, because the statement is there too openly: Look sexy, blonde!"

"One shouldn't know at first whether she is sexy or not."

"I'm very shy when it comes to women."

Women played an important role in Hitchcock's life and career. His wife, Alma, worked closely with him; his daughter, Patricia, appeared in three of his films: *Stage Fright, Strangers on a Train,* and *Psycho*; Hitchcock's personal assistant, from *Under Capricorn* in 1949 until the end of his career, was a woman named Peggy Robertson. Hitchcock also worked closely with Joan Harrison. He once told screenwriter Charles Bennett that there were only two women he ever could have married: "Alma, whom I did, and Joan, whom I didn't." Harrison cowrote *Jamaica Inn* and *Rebecca*, both based on Daphne Du Maurier novels, as well as *Foreign Correspondent, Suspicion,* and *Saboteur*. She also worked with the director on his famous television show "Alfred Hitchcock Presents." Hitchcock worked with three other women screenwriters aside from his wife and Joan Harrison: Dorothy Parker, who cowrote *Saboteur* with Peter Viertel and Joan Harrison; Sally Benson, who cowrote *Shadow of a Doubt* with Thornton Wilder and Alma Reville; and Jay Presson Allen, who replaced Evan Hunter (*The Birds*) on *Marnie*. Edith Head, the famous costume designer, was yet another important and influential woman in Hitchcock's career. They worked for the first time in 1946 on *Notorious*, and Edith Head continued to collaborate with Hitchcock on most of his movies until the last one, *Family Plot*, in 1976.

But perhaps the director's most important collaborators were his actresses. No one can reflect on Alfred Hitchcock without immediately thinking of Grace Kelly, Tippi Hedren, Joan Fontaine, Janet Leigh, Ingrid Bergman, Kim Novak, Doris Day, and Eva Marie Saint, and vice versa. Blondes or brunettes, they became part of his universe, and his approach to these characters reveals that Hitchcock fulfilled, through the women in his films, his wildest fantasies. He transformed them just as James Stewart in *Vertigo* changes Kim Novak back into the woman he once loved and thinks he lost.

Hitchcock was admittedly very shy when it came to women. Women intrigued him; he liked to make them mysterious in his films and revealed to the audience, with the help of a plot and a male costar, his own definition of what a woman is, or should be. In a sense, most of the Hitchcockian heroines are strong, but along the way, oftentimes and thanks to a man, the audience discovers that it is all a cover, or a seduction device. In several of his films, the woman characters are weak and are introduced as victims. However, and again because of their association with a man, they completely change into strong, assertive women. But in both cases, according to Hitchcock, women need men to realize themselves and to give a meaning to their life. Is this a sexist attitude? Hitchcock has been accused of being a misogynist on many occasions, but his attitude toward women is more complex than that. Hitchcock had an obsessive personality and many fantasy romances, and in real life, an infatuation with many different women, including actress Tippi Hedren. In all fairness, his ambiguous treatment of the heroines in his films could simply have been another way for Hitchcock to create an additional level of suspense as well as another trick to shock his audience.

Women Insulting Men

The Lady Vanishes
IRIS HENDERSON [Margaret Lockwood] (*to* GILBERT [Michael Redgrave]): Yes, you heartless, callous, selfish, swollen-headed beast, you.

Foreign Correspondent
CAROL FISHER [Laraine Day] (*to* JOHNNY JONES [Joel McCrea]): Look, your childish mind is as out of place in Europe as you are in my bedroom.

CAROL (*to* JOHNNY): All you're interested in is having fun with windmills and bathrooms.

Suspicion
JOHNNY AYSGARTH [Cary Grant]: What do you think of me by contrast to your horse?
LINA MCLAIDLAW [Joan Fontaine]: I think that if I ever got the bit between your teeth, I would have no trouble in handling you at all.

Saboteur
PAT MARTIN [Priscilla Lane] (*to* BARRY KANE [Robert Cummings]): You look like a saboteur. You have a saboteur's disposition.

Notorious
ALICIA HUBERMAN [Ingrid Bergman] (*to* DEVLIN [Cary Grant]): I don't like gentlemen who grin at me.

ALICIA (*to* DEVLIN): You double-crossing buzzard. You're a cop!

The Paradine Case
JUDY FLAQUER [Joan Tetzel] (*referring to* ANTHONY KEANE [Gregory Peck]): Men are such horrible beasts.

Rear Window
LISA FREEMONT [Grace Kelly] (*referring to a neighbor entertaining men*): I'd say she is doing a woman's hardest job: juggling wolves.

To Catch a Thief
FRANCES STEVENS [Grace Kelly]: You're somewhat egotistical.
JOHN ROBIE [Cary Grant]: Fighting fire with fire.

"If you're going to kill someone, do it simply."
Cary Grant discusses murder over dinner in *Suspicion*.

The Trouble With Harry

JENNIFER ROGERS [Shirley MacLaine] (*referring to* HARRY, *her dead husband*): He was...horribly good.

The Birds

MELANIE DANIELS [Tippi Hedren] (*to* MITCH BRENNER [Rod Taylor]): I think you're a louse!

MITCH: You like me, uh?
MELANIE: I loathe you. You have no manners. And you're arrogant and conceited and—I wrote a letter about it in fact, but I tore it up.

ANNIE HAYWORTH [Suzanne Pleshette]: Maybe there's never been anything between Mitch and any girl.

Marnie

MARNIE EDGAR [Tippi Hedren] (*to* MARK RUTLAND [Sean Connery]): Oh, men! You say, "No, thanks," to one of them and bingo, you're a candidate for the funny farm. It would be hilarious if it weren't pathetic!

MARNIE: Women are weak and feeble, and men are filthy pigs!

MARNIE (*to* MARK): Talk about dream worlds! You've got a pathological fix on a woman who's not only an admitted criminal but who screams if you come near her.

Frenzy

FELIX FORSYTHE [Bernard Cribbins] (*referring to one of his employees*, RICHARD BLANEY [Jon Finch]): Quite apart from the fact that half the time he's pulling your tits instead of pulling pints.
BABS MILLIGAN [Anna Massey]: Now, look here!

FELIX: He can't keep his hands off you! The customers are always talking about it!

BABS: And what about you? Always fingering me!

Hitchcock's Women

The Lodger (title cards)

In *The Lodger*, DAISY BUNTING [June] can't believe that the man (Ivor Novello) she loves is a killer:
He's innocent! He's innocent!

And later:
You're shivering. Keep your handcuffs hidden and we'll get some brandy.

Blackmail

THE ARTIST [Cyril Ritchard]: You are frightened.

ALICE WHITE [Anny Ondra]: I'm certainly not. It takes more than a man to frighten me.

THE ARTIST: Yeah, that's what I thought.

Murder!

DIANA BARING [Norah Baring] (*referring to her death sentence*): If they want to do the other thing, they can. I fought it and got over it except at night. It will be no worse than the dentist.

The 39 Steps

ANNABELLA SMITH [Lucie Mannheim]: Listen, I'm gonna tell you something which is not very healthy to know, but now that they've followed me here, you're in it as much as I am.

ANNABELLA (*to* RICHARD HANNAY [Robert Donat]): Clear out, Hannay; they'll get you next!

PAMELA [Madeleine Carroll] (*to* HANNAY): I feel such a fool not having believed you.

HANNAY: Beautiful, mysterious woman pursued by gunmen. Sounds like a spy story.
ANNABELLA: It's exactly what it is, only I prefer the word "agent" better.

The Lady Vanishes
IRIS HENDERSON [Margaret Lockwood]: Then you are a spy.
MISS FROY [Dame May Witty]: I always think that's such a grim word.

MISS FROY: My name's Froy.
IRIS: Did you say Freud?
MISS FROY: No, "o-y." No "e-u-d." Froy.

Secret Agent
RICHARD ASHENDEN [John Gielgud]: Look here, what did you pick that job for?
ELSA CARRINGTON [Madeleine Carroll]: What else was there to do?
RICHARD: All sorts of things. You could have been a nurse or something.
ELSA: Me? I'm no ministering angel!

Rebecca
In *Rebecca*, both the novel by Daphne Du Maurier and the film version, SHE, the character played by Joan Fontaine, a shy, vulnerable, and naive creature slowly becomes a strong woman:

We can never go back to Manderley again; that much is certain. But sometimes, in my dreams, I do go back to the strange days of my life which began for me in the South of France.

(*referring to her father, who painted the same tree over and over*): You see, he had a theory that if you should find one perfect thing, place, or person, you should stick to it.

You know, I wish there could be an invention that bottled up the memory, like perfume, that never fainted, never got stained, and whenever I wanted to, I could uncork the bottle and live the memory all over again.

Oh, I wish I were a woman of thirty-six dressed in black satin with a string of pearls.

(*referring to the deceased* REBECCA): Every day, I realize the things that she had and that I lack; beauty and wit and intelligence and all the things that are so important in a woman.

How do you do? I'm Maxim's wife.

I am Mrs. de Winter now.

(*to* MAXIM DE WINTER [Laurence Olivier]): Rebecca's dead. That's what we got to remember. Rebecca's dead.

   In *Rebecca*, MRS. DANVERS [Judith Anderson], the house-keeper, simply adores REBECCA and wants to destroy the second Mrs. de Winter:
MRS. DANVERS (*to* SHE *and referring to* REBECCA's *sexy nightgown*): Look, you can see my hand through it.

Do you think the dead come back and watch the livings?

I watched you go down just as I watched her a year ago. Even in the same dress, you could not compare.

You thought you could be Mrs. de Winter. Live in her house,

walk in her steps, take the things that were hers, but she is too strong for you. You can't fight her. No one ever got the better of her, never, never. She was beaten in the end, but it wasn't a man, it wasn't a woman, it was the sea.

SHE (*to her husband*, MAXIM DE WINTER): Mrs. Danvers, she's gone mad. She said she'd rather destroy Manderley than see us happy here.

Suspicion

In *Suspicion*, Joan Fontaine portrays LINA MCLAIDLAW, a character similar to the one she played in *Rebecca*, who is married to the suspicious but seductive JOHNNY AYSGARTH [Cary Grant]:
I may seem provincial, but frankly, I don't understand men like you... You always give me the feeling that you're laughing at me.

I must be a novelty by contrast with the women that you're photographed with.

Anyway, if my father saw me come in both late and beautiful, he might have a stroke.

Johnny, I think I'm beginning to understand you. You're a big baby.

Let's turn back, Johnny. Let's go home and see it all through together.

This is as much my fault as yours. I was only thinking of myself, not what you were going through. If I had been really close to you, you could have confided in me, but you were afraid, ashamed to come to me.

To Catch a Thief

In *To Catch a Thief*, FRANCES STEVENS [Grace Kelly] makes a similar revelation to JOHN ROBIE [Cary Grant]:

Were you afraid to admit that you can't just do everything by yourself and that you needed the help of a good woman and that you just aren't the lone wolf you think you are.

Saboteur

PAT MARTIN [Priscilla Lane]: It's a free country, a girl can change her mind, can't she?

Strangers on a Train

MIRIAM HAINES [Laura Elliot]: Woman's privilege to change her mind.

Shadow of a Doubt

In *Shadow of a Doubt*, CHARLIE [Teresa Wright] is a bored young girl, infatuated with her uncle CHARLIE [Joseph Cotten], who is in fact a dangerous killer:

I'm perfectly well. I've just been thinking for hours. I come to the conclusion that I give up. I simply give up.

Do you ever stop to think that a family should be the most wonderful thing in the world and that this family has simply gone to pieces.

I've become a nagging old maid.

I guess I don't like to be an average girl in an average family.

I know a wonderful person who will come and shake us all up. Just the one to save us.

He'll come for me. I'm named after him.

"My uncle hasn't done anything. He knows it would kill my mother if he did."

Teresa Wright with her uncle, Joseph Cotten, and her mother, Patricia Collinge, in *Shadow of a Doubt*.

We're not just an uncle and a niece. It's something else. I know you. I know you don't tell people a lot of things. I don't, either. I have the feeling that inside you somewhere there is something nobody knows about.

But we're sort of like twins, don't you see?

Did you see the way they looked at you? I bet they wondered who you are. Oh, Uncle Charlie, I love to walk with you. I want everybody to see you.

It's funny, but when I try to think of how I feel, I always come back to Uncle Charlie.

Go away or I'll kill myself. See, that's the way I feel about you.

ANN NEWTON [Edna May Wonacott] (CHARLIE's *bratty younger sister*): I wish I had been born in the South. Southern women have such class. They pick flowers with gloves on.

Lifeboat
CONSTANCE PORTER [Tallulah Bankhead]: You know I'm practically immortal, Ritt.

Spellbound
CONSTANCE PETERSEN [Ingrid Bergman]: I've always loved very feminine clothes but never quite dared to wear them. But I'm going to after this. I'm going to wear exactly the things that please me.

Notorious
ALICIA HUBERMAN [Ingrid Bergman] (*to* DEVLIN [Cary Grant]): Go away and leave me alone. I have my own life to live. Good times! That's what I want and laugh with people I like and no underhanded cops who will put me in a shooting gallery... but people of my own kind who will treat me right and like me and understand me.

ALICIA's comments before and after the suicide of her father, a traitor and a spy: Now I remember how nice he was. How nice we both were. Very nice. It's a very curious feeling. As if something had happened to me and not to him. You see, I don't have to hate him anymore, or myself.

ALICIA (*to* DEVLIN): Why won't you let me be happy?

DEVLIN: You enjoy making fun of me, don't you?

"You've always been jealous of any women I've shown any interest in."

Claude Rains is caught between his evil mother, Leopoldine Konstantin, and his wife, Ingrid Bergman, who turns out to be a spy in *Notorious*.

ALICIA: No, Dev. I'm making fun of myself. I'm pretending I'm a nice, unspoiled child whose heart is full of daisies and buttercups.

The Paradine Case

LADY HORFIELD [Ethel Barrymore] (*referring to* MRS. PARADINE [Valli], *a woman who has murdered her husband*): I do pity her. Who needs pity more than a woman who sinned?

GAY KEANE [Ann Todd] (*to her husband,* ANTHONY [Gregory Peck], *after he discovers that the woman he is defending—and loves—is a murderess*): The most important day of your life is now.

Rope
JANET WALKER [Joan Chandler]: You couldn't know me these days. I'm a new woman. Punctual as a clock.
MRS. ATWATER [Constance Collier]: That's very unfeminine, my dear!

MRS. ATWATER (*referring to Cary Grant in Notorious*): He was thrilling in that new thing with Bergman. What was it called, now? The something of the something. No, that was the other one. This is just plain something!

Under Capricorn
In *Under Capricorn*, Ingrid Bergman is LADY HENRIETTA FLUSKY, a woman who is disillusioned with both her life and herself:
I told you I'm finished.

I had courage long ago, but I lost it.

My best isn't much good.

Stage Fright
EVE GILL [Jane Wyman]: I'll make her talk. It will be one woman to another.
COMMODORE GILL, her father [Alastair Sim]: An impressive situation at any time.

EVE (*referring to* CHARLOTTE INWOOD [Marlene Dietrich], *whom she suspects is a murderess*): Who knows what goes on in a woman's mind? I don't know.

In *Stage Fright*, Marlene Dietrich portrays the rather obnoxious—but curiously endearing—CHARLOTTE INWOOD:

We can stand so much of detectives. After all, they're only policemen with smaller feet.

I hope you're not going to turn into one of those explicit people who always tell you exactly how they feel when you ask them.

I hate rainy funerals!

CHARLOTTE: Darling! Whatever happened to that peculiar figure of yours?
EVE: It's a new dress, madam.
CHARLOTTE: Keep it, dear. What it does to you is worth thousands.
EVE: I bought it at a sale.
CHARLOTTE: Don't confide in me, just pour me some tea, will you.

I Confess
RUTH GRANDFORT [Anne Baxter]: I was going to help Michael, was I? I destroyed him.

Dial M for Murder
MARGOT WENDICE [Grace Kelly]: You know how I hate doing nothing.

MARGOT: I don't like thrillers when I'm alone.

Rear Window
In *Rear Window*, in order to get her boyfriend's, L. B. JEFFRIES [James Stewart], attention, LISA FREEMONT [Grace Kelly] decides to help him solve a murder:
I'm going to make this a week you'll never forget.

Let's start from the beginning again, Jeff. Tell me everything you saw and what you think it means...

Surprise is the most important element of attack.

I'm not much on rear-window ethics.

Jeff, if you're squeamish, don't look.

Women aren't that predictable.

LISA: I wish I could be creative.
JEFFRIES: Sweetie, you are. You have a great talent for creating difficult situations.

In *Rear Window*, Thelma Ritter portrays STELLA, a wise-cracking nurse:
STELLA: Oh, dear, we've become a race of Peeping Toms.

STELLA (*referring to* JEFFRIES's *camera*): Mind if I use that portable keyhole.

JEFFRIES (*referring to the man he suspects of murder*): What was his reaction when he looked at the note?
STELLA: It was not the kind of an expression that would get him a quick loan at the bank!

To Catch a Thief
FRANCES STEVENS [Grace Kelly]: I bet you snored around her; the big, handsome lumberman from America. I bet you told him all your trees were Sequoias. (Are we to understand from this remark that John Robie [Cary Grant] has an "over-inflated" image of his attributes?)

JOHN: Where were you born?
FRANCES: In a taxi. Between home and the hospital.

The Trouble With Harry
JENNIFER ROGERS [Shirley MacLaine] (*referring to the fact that*

she has to wash her dead husband's clothes): Isn't it odd? After refusing for so long, here I am finally doing Harry's laundry!

The Man Who Knew Too Much (1956)

JO MCKENNA [Doris Day]: You don't know anything about this man, and he knows everything there is to know about you.

The Wrong Man

In *The Wrong Man*, ROSE BALESTRERO [Vera Miles] loses her mind after her husband, MANNY [Henry Fonda] is accused of crimes he didn't commit:

Don't you see, it doesn't do any good to care. No matter what you do, they've got it fixed. No matter how innocent you are or how hard you try, they'll find you guilty.

It's true, Manny. There's something wrong with me. You'll have to let them put me away somewhere.

Vertigo

MADELEINE ELSTER [Kim Novak]: If I'm mad, that would explain it, wouldn't it?

There is someone within me, and she says I must die.

MIDGE WOOD [Barbara Bel Geddes]: I have music for dipsomaniacs, music for melancholiacs, music for hypochondriacs. I wonder what would happen if someone got their files mixed up.

Psycho

MARION CRANE [Janet Leigh] (*to her boyfriend,* SAM LOOMIS [John Gavin]): You make respectability sound—disrespectful.

MARION CRANE: I stepped into a private trap back there. I'd like to go back and try to pull myself out of it.

LILA CRANE [Vera Miles] (MARION's *sister*): Patience doesn't run in my family, Sam.

The Birds
ANNIE HAYWORTH [Suzanne Pleshette]: I'm an open book, I'm afraid. Or rather a closed one.

MELANIE DANIELS [Tippi Hedren]: I'm neither poor nor innocent.

In *The Birds*, MELANIE DANIELS [Tippi Hedren] is a strong woman who likes to challenge men like Mitch Brenner [Rod Taylor]:
MITCH: What do you want?
MELANIE: I thought you knew. I want to go through life laughing and jumping into fountains naked! Good night!

MITCH: You have a job?
MELANIE: I have several jobs.
MITCH: What do you do?
MELANIE: On Mondays and Wednesdays, I work at the Travelers Aid at the airport.
MITCH: Helping travelers?
MELANIE: No, misguiding them. I thought you could read my character.

In *The Birds*, a WOMAN [Doreen Lang] accuses MELANIE of being the cause of the birds' attacks:
Why are they doing this? Why are they doing this? They said when you got here the whole thing started. Who are you? What are you? Where did you come from? I think you're the cause of all this. I think you're evil! Evil!

Marnie
In *Marnie*, Tippi Hedren portrays a disturbed woman:
MARNIE EDGAR: I don't believe in luck.

MARK RUTLAND [Sean Connery]: What do you believe in?
MARNIE: Nothing. Oh, horses, maybe. At least they're beautiful and nothing in this world like people.

We don't need men, Mama. We can do very well for ourselves.

I didn't say men weren't interested in me. I said I wasn't interested in them.

The colors, stop the colors!

MARK: Why the hell didn't you jump over the side?
MARNIE: The idea was to kill myself, not feed the damn fish.

Oh, help me! Oh, God, somebody help me!

(*to her horse*): Oh, Forio, if you want to bite somebody, bite me.

Decent. Oh, Mama, you surely realized your ambition. I certainly am decent. Of course, I'm a cheat and a liar and a thief, but I am decent.

MARNIE (*after killing her horse and remembering killing a sailor*): There—there now.

Hitchcock Believed in Women's Intuition

Rear Window
LISA FREEMONT [Grace Kelly]: I'll trade you my feminine intuition for a bed for the night.

Frenzy
In *Frenzy*, MRS. OXFORD [Vivien Merchant] portrays the wife of the inspector in charge of a murder case:

I told you it wasn't Blaney. Didn't I tell you were on the wrong track? Woman's intuition is worth more than all those laboratories. I can't think why you don't teach it in police colleges.

In both *The Lady Vanishes* and *Frenzy* we have a woman describing accurately another person, proving that women in Hitchcock's films have an eye for details...

The Lady Vanishes

GILBERT EDMAN [Michael Redgrave]: What was she wearing?
IRIS HENDERSON [Margaret Lockwood]: Tweeds, oatmeal flecked with brown, a three-quarter coat with patch pockets, a scarf, felt hat, brown shoes, a tussore shirt, and...and a small blue handkerchief in the breast pocket. I can't remember any more.
GILBERT (*sarcastic*): You couldn't have been paying attention.

Frenzy

INSPECTOR OXFORD [Alec McCowen]: Miss Barling, could you describe Mr. Blaney for us, what he looked like, what he was wearing?
MONICA BARLING [Jean Marsh] (the secretary in a matrimonial agency): Well, yes, I think I can. He was a man in his thirties about an inch or so and a six foot tall. He had dark hair, green eyes, a mustache. I estimate his weight is about one hundred and fifty-five pounds. He was wearing a rather old-fashioned jacket with leather patches on the shoulders and at the elbows. In my opinion, it was quite unsuitable for London. He was also carrying a raincoat.
INSPECTOR OXFORD: It's an extraordinarily precise description, Miss Barling.
MONICA: In my job, I've learned to keep a sharp eye on men, Inspector.

Dial M for Mother

A cousin of Alfred Hitchcock's had this to say about Emma Jane Whelan, the director's mother:

Emma Hitchcock was a smartly dressed, sedate person, very quietly spoken with an aristocratic manner. She was very meticulous when preparing a meal, at which she was very good. She would not venture out of her room unless neatly, perfectly dressed, and she quietly conducted her affairs in a dignified manner.

This description almost matches that given by the director of himself. Hitchcock once declared: "I am a creature of habit and order." Toward the end of his life, Hitchcock also said: "Well, you could say I am a very gentle soul. A man who wouldn't hurt a flea. A very unobtrusive man who likes to blend into the background." Hitchcock, like his mother, was somewhat of a loner, always impeccably dressed and fussy about his appearance: "I like nothing but white shirts," he said, "except for TV, when they may have to be blue. And no jewelry of any kind, not even a wristwatch. My aim is quiet dignity." Hitchcock also declared: "You see, I'm a very fastidious man, and I like a very strong semblance of order in my life. I'm one of the most meticulous, orderly people you'll ever meet."

Emma Jane Whelan was born in 1863 and came from an

Irish Catholic background. In 1887, she married William Hitchcock, who was twenty-four and a year her senior. William owned a grocery business, and after three years of marriage, he and Emma had their first child, William, Jr. In 1892, they had a daughter, Ellen Kathleen, who was immediately nicknamed Nellie, and in 1899, Alfred Joseph was born.

Donald Spoto explains in insightful biography *The Dark Side of Genius: The Life of Alfred Hitchcock* that throughout his life the director rarely talked about his mother, even though he was always very intimate with her. As a child, Hitchcock would come home at night and stand at his mom's bed to answer her questions about his day. When his father died, Alfred Hitchcock was fifteen; he immediately found a job and became even closer to his mother. Even in his adult life, Hitchcock's mom would often accompany her son and his wife on their vacations. Emma Hitchcock was also a stubborn woman, which is yet something else her youngest son shares in common with her. When Hitchcock moved with his wife from England to America in 1939 not only to direct *Rebecca* but to establish his permanent residency in California, Emma refused to leave her roots despite her son's insistence. In 1942, Hitchcock directed *Shadow of a Doubt*, which he always referred to as his favorite among all his films. In it, Teresa Wright's mother's name is Emma, just like Hitchcock's. It is rather ironic that the director received the news of his mother's death during the shooting of *Shadow of a Doubt*.

Aside from a few isolated cases, for example, *Shadow of a Doubt*, mothers in Hitchcock's films are either manipulative, castrative, evil, or dominating—or all of the above at once. Even though mothers were secondary characters in Hitchcock's movies, they were an important and pivotal factor in the stories. The quotes in this chapter demonstrate that Hitchcock acknowledged the influence of one's family heritage as a determining element in life. Some of his female characters have a motherly attitude toward the men they seduce, while most of the mother characters use their power to change the fate of their children, relatives, friends, and enemies alike for better—or worse.

Women Being Motherly Toward Men

Spellbound

DR. FLEUROT [John Emery] (*to* CONSTANCE PETERSEN [Ingrid Bergman]): Last night at dinner, a dimple appeared in your cheek that was never there before, and I detected the outcroppings of a mother's instinct toward Dr. Edwards.

CONSTANCE (*referring to the man she loves*): What can I do for him?
DR. ALEX BRULOV [Michael Chekhov]: Ah, you're not his mother; you're an analyst.

Notorious

ALICIA HUBERMAN [Ingrid Bergman] (*to* DEVLIN [Cary Grant]): Well, handsome, you better tell Mama what's going on.

Vertigo

MIDGE WOOD [Barbara Bel Geddes]: Why don't you go away for a while?
JOHN SCOTTIE FERGUSON [James Stewart]: You mean to forget? Oh, no, Midge, don't be so motherly. I'm not gonna crack up.

MIDGE (to John who is having a mental breakdown): You're not lost. Mother is here.

JOHN: What's this doohickey?
MIDGE: It's a brassiere. You know about those things. You're a big boy now.

North by Northwest
ROGER O. THORNHILL [Cary Grant]: When I was a little boy, I wouldn't even let my mother undress me.
EVE KENDALL [Eva Marie Saint]: You're a big boy now.

Mothers

The Lodger (title card)
A MOTHER TO HER SON [Ivor Novello]: Swear to me, my son, you will not rest until the AVENGER has been brought to justice.

Foreign Correspondent
MRS. JONES [Dorothy Vaughan] (*referring to her son's new hat*): Don't wear it over one eye like that. It makes you look like a gangster.

Suspicion
MRS. MCLAIDLAW [Dame May Whitty] (*referring to her daughter*): I'm afraid she is rather spinsterish.

Shadow of a Doubt
EMMA NEWTON [Patricia Collinge]: My goodness, the way men do things.

And later, referring to her brother:
Oh, you mean, what does he do? He is just in business, the way men are.

Notorious
MADAME SEBASTIAN [Leopoldine Konstantin]: Wouldn't it be a little too much if we were both going to turn like idiots?
ALEXANDER SEBASTIAN [Claude Rains] her son: Please, Mother, I want to enjoy myself.
MADAME SEBASTIAN: Is it so boring to sit with me alone?
ALEXANDER: Not at all.

MADAME SEBASTIAN (*to her son, referring to the fact that he married an undercover American agent*): You are protected by the enormity of your stupidity.

And later:

You're almost as impetuous as before your wedding. You barred me from that episode. Let me arrange this one.

MADAME SEBASTIAN (*to* ALICIA HUBERMAN [Ingrid Bergman]): Alex has always admired you. Now at last I know why.

Stage Fright

MRS. GILL [Sybil Thorndike] (*referring to her daughter*): I can't understand why that girl is so late. I mean, she is always so punctual. She takes that from me. Her father is not punctual at all. I mean, he catches trains and things, but always at the last moment. I'm always at least an hour before.

Strangers on a Train

MRS. ANTHONY [Marion Lorne] (*to her son, a disturbed killer who has just strangled a woman*): I do wish you'd keep your hands quiet. You're so restless lately.

BRUNO ANTHONY [Robert Walker]: I like them to look just right.

MRS. ANTHONY: Did I file them too short?

BRUNO: Oh, no, Mother, just fine. Thanks.

MRS. ANTHONY: What's the matter?

BRUNO: Oh, I'm all right. Don't worry about me.

MRS. ANTHONY: But you look so pale, dear. Are you out of vitamins?

BRUNO: I took a bottle yesterday, Ma. A whole fifth.

MRS. ANTHONY: Oh, but you have that look, dear. I always can tell. Now, you haven't been doing anything foolish?...Well, I do hope you've forgotten about that silly little plan of yours.

BRUNO: Which one?

MRS. ANTHONY: About blowing up the White House.

BRUNO: Oh, Ma, I was only fooling. Besides, what would the President say?

MRS. ANTHONY: You're a naughty boy, Bruno. You could always make me laugh.

MRS. ANTHONY: Bruno, I do wish you'd take up painting. Such a soothing pastime.

To Catch a Thief

JESSIE STEVENS [Jessie Royce Landis] (*referring to her daughter,* FRANCES [Grace Kelly]): I'm sorry I ever sent her to that finishing school. I think they finished her there.

FRANCES: Mother, this is why I've had to spend half my life traveling around the world after you, to keep men like this away from you.

JESSIE: Well, after this, let me run my own interference. Looks like the blockers are having all the fun.

JESSIE: Just what did he steal from you?

FRANCES: Oh, Mother!

JESSIE: Sit down while I tell you about life and John Robie. Sit down before I knock you out.

The Trouble With Harry

JENNIFER ROGERS [Shirley MacLaine] (*referring to her son*): You'll never make sense out of Arnie. He's got his own timing.

The Wrong Man

MRS. BALESTRERO [Esther Minciotti] (*referring to her son*): I wouldn't worry about Manny, Rose. I used to worry sometimes, but that's just because he is so steady. You . . . you never expect him to be late.

North by Northwest

CLARA THORNHILL [Jessie Royce Landis] (*to her son*): I don't see why you want me along.
ROGER O. THORNHILL [Cary Grant]: You have an air of respectability."
CLARA: Don't be sarcastic, Roger.

CLARA: Roger, I think we should go.
ROGER: Don't be so nervous.
CLARA: I'm not nervous; I'll be late for the bridge club.
ROGER: Good, you'll lose less than usual.

CLARA: I think I'd like to meet these killers.

CLARA: You gentlemen aren't really trying to kill my son.

Psycho

MRS. BATES: No! I tell you no! I won't have you bringing strange young girls in here for supper by candlelight, I suppose, in the cheap, erotic fashion of young men with cheap, erotic minds!
NORMAN BATES, her son [Anthony Perkins]: Mother, please!
MRS. BATES: And then what after supper? Music? Whispers?
NORMAN: Mother, she's just a stranger! She's hungry, and it's raining out.
MRS. BATES: Mother, she's just a stranger! As if men don't desire strangers! Ah! I refuse to speak of disgusting things, because they disgust me! Do you understand, boy?

MRS. BATES: It is sad when a mother has to speak the words that condemn her own son. I can't allow them to think I would commit murder. Put him away now, as I should have years ago. He was always bad, and in the end he intended to tell them I killed those girls and that man, as if I could do anything but just sit and stare like one of his stuffed birds.

They know I can't move a finger, and I want to just sit here and be quiet just in case they suspect me. They are probably watching me—well, let them. Let them see what kind of person I am—not even going to swat that fly. I hope that they are watching. They will see; they will see, and they will say, "why, she wouldn't even harm a fly."

The Birds
MITCH BRENNER [Rod Taylor]: I think I can handle Melanie Daniels by myself.
LYDIA BRENNER [Jessica Tandy]: Well...as long as you know what you want, Mitch?
MITCH: I know exactly what I want, Mother.

LYDIA (*to* MELANIE DANIELS [Tippi Hedren]): What's the matter with all the birds?

I wish I was a stronger person.

Mitch has always done exactly what he wanted to do.

I don't know what I'd do if Mitch weren't here.

LYDIA: I don't even know if I...like you or not.
MELANIE: Is that so important, Mrs. Brenner, you liking me?
LYDIA: Well, yes, I think so. Mitch is important to me. I want to like whatever girl he chooses.
MELANIE: And perhaps if you don't?
LYDIA: Well, I don't think it will matter to anyone but me.

Marnie
BERNICE EDGAR [Louise Latham] (*to her daughter,* MARNIE [Tippi Hedren]): Too blond hair always looks like a woman is trying to attract the men. Men and a good name don't go together.

"I never wanted to have the obvious blonde, the one who has her sex hanging around her neck like jewelry, the big-bosomed girl. Neither the Marilyn Monroe nor the Jean Harlow type was for me, because the statement is there too openly—Look sexy blonde!" —Alfred Hitchcock.

Tippi Hedren portrayed the typical Hitchcockian heroine in *The Birds*.

Regarding his cameo appearances, Hitchcock declared: "It all started with a shortage of extras in my first thriller [*The Lodger*]. I was in for a few seconds as an editor with my back to the camera. It wasn't really much, but I played it to a hilt. Since then I have been trying to get into everyone of my pictures. It isn't that I like the business, but it has an impelling fascination that I can't resist. When I do it, the cast, the grips, and the cameramen and everyone else gather to make it as difficult as possible for me. But I can't stop now."

Hitchcock and his two dogs in *The Birds*.

BERNICE: Decent women don't have any need for any men. Look at you. Marnie. I told Mrs. Cotten, "Look at my girl Marnie, she's too smart to get herself mixed up with men. None of them!"

BERNICE (*to her daughter*): You're the only thing in this world I ever did love.

What They Said About Mothers

The Lady Vanishes
MARGARET [Linden Travers] (*to her married lover,* MR. TODHUN TER [Cecil Parker] *and referring to her husband*): Robert thinks I'm cruising with mother.

Mr. and Mrs. Smith
ANN SMITH [Carole Lombard] (*to her husband,* DAVID [Robert Montgomery]): I've always had a suspicion about you. So did my mother. Your forehead slants back too much.

ANN: Yes, Mother. Things come to worse, I'll spend the night with you.

CHUCK BENSON [Jack Carson] (*to* DAVID SMITH): You know what I can't understand? Whenever two people have a fight, the woman always goes home to her mother, and when my wife and I have a fight, I have to get out of the house.

Suspicion
JOHNNY AYSGARTH [Cary Grant] (*to his wife,* LINA MCLAIDLAW [Joan Fontaine]): You're still annoyed with me, aren't you?
LINA: No, Johnny, really. I still don't feel well, that's all.
JOHNNY: And a few days at your mother's house will do you more good than staying at home.

Shadow of a Doubt

CHARLIE NEWTON [Teresa Wright]: Poor mother. She works like a dog, just like a dog.

JOE NEWTON, [Henry Travers] her father: Where is she?

CHARLIE: She's out. When she comes back, it will be the same thing: dinner, then dishes, then bed. I don't see how she stands it. You know, she is really a wonderful woman. I mean, she is not just a mother, and I think we ought to do something for her. Don't you think we should?

JOE: Yeah, what were you thinking of doing for her?

CHARLIE: Nothing, I suppose. I guess we'll just have to wait for a miracle or something.

CHARLIE (*to* JACK GRAHAM [Macdonald Carey], *a detective*): My uncle hasn't done anything. He knows it would kill my mother if he did.

UNCLE CHARLIE OAKLEY [Joseph Cotten] (*a killer who uses psychological blackmail on his niece* CHARLIE *by referring to her mother, who is also his own sister, in order to keep her from denouncing him*): Think of your mother. It will kill your mother.

CHARLIE: Yes, it will kill my mother. Take your few days. See that you get away from here.

CHARLIE: I wish I'd told my mother about you. I wish I had.

UNCLE CHARLIE: I know what you're thinking. How do you think your mother would have felt. What would it do to her now?

CHARLIE: I don't want you here, Uncle Charlie. I don't want you to touch my mother.

UNCLE CHARLIE after CHARLIE finally succeeds in making him leave town: I want you to know I think you were right to make me leave. It was best for your mother. Best for all of us. You saw what happened to her last night. She is not very strong, you know. I don't think she could stand the shock.

EMMA NEWTON [Patricia Collinge] (CHARLIE's *mother and* UN CLE CHARLIE's *sister, referring to a picture taken of her brother as a child*): It was taken the very day he had his accident. And then, a few days later, when the pictures came home, Mama cried. She wondered if he'd ever look the same. She wondered if he'd ever be the same.

ANN NEWTON [Edna May Wonacott] is CHARLIE's young, bratty sister: Really, Papa, you'd think Mama had never seen a phone. She makes no allowance for science. She thinks she has to cover the distance by sheer lung power.

JOE: How is your mother, Herb?
HERB HAWKINS [Hume Cronyn], a middle-aged man who still lives with his mother and is a friend and a neighbor of the Newton family: Oh, uh, just meddling.
   And a few days later:
EMMA: Well, Herb, how is your mother?
HERB: Oh, she's just meddling.

Spellbound
LIEUTENANT COOLEY [Art Baker] (*referring to his mother's health*): Oh, she is still complaining about rheumatism. She figures I ought to be transferred down to Florida. I said, do you expect me to sacrifice all chance of promotion just because you've got rheumatism?
   And later:
COOLEY (*referring to his boss*): He gave me some crack about being a mama's boy.

Rope
JANET WALKER [Joan Chandler]: How is Mrs. Kentley?

"Murder is a crime for most men..."
"...but a privilege for the few."

From left: John Dall, James Stewart, and Farley Granger in *Rope*.

MR. KENTLEY [Sir Cedric Hardwicke]: As usual...It's a cold
this time. I hope David arrives soon. She wants him to call
her...

JANET: David is her only son, Mr. Kentley.

MR. KENTLEY: He is my only child, too, but I'm willing to let
him grow up.

Notorious

ALEXANDER SEBASTIAN [Claude Rains] (*to his mother*): You've
always been jealous of any women I've shown any interest in.

The Paradine Case

GAY KEANE [Ann Todd]: I remember the first time you called on me with two tickets for the first night to that short play and you had forgotten to dress. The look of horror on Mother's face as we left the house. It took her five years to forgive that parting look.

ANTHONY KEANE [Gregory Peck]: It took her fifty years to perfect that look.

Stage Fright

EVE GILL [Jane Wyman]: My mother is really a dear. My father, too, of course, but they shout at one another, and none of them like to shout.

COMMODORE GILL [Alastair Sim]: But I never hoped of being appreciated. Yes, your mother cured me of that. That's why I could never be bothered with your mother.

CHARLOTTE INWOOD [Marlene Dietrich]: I had a dog once. He hated me. At last, he bit me, and I had him shot. When I give all my love and I get back treachery and hatred, it's as if my mother had struck me in the face.

Strangers on a Train

BRUNO ANTHONY [Robert Walker] (*referring to the tie clip that bears his name*): You probably think it's corny, but my mother gave it to me, so I wear it to please her.

BRUNO: Don't worry, I'm not going to shoot you, Mr. Haines. It might disturb Mother.

BRUNO: I'm afraid that Mother wasn't very much help, was she? Well, you know she hasn't been well for a long time. She is a little, how should you say, confused. Poor mother.

Psycho

NORMAN BATES [Anthony Perkins]: Uh-uh, Mother-m-mother, uh—what is the phrase? She isn't quite herself today.

To Catch a Thief

FRANCES STEVENS [Grace Kelly]: All evening long, you only looked at my mother, never at me.

JOHN ROBIE [Cary Grant]: I kissed you, didn't I?

FRANCES: I kissed you.

JOHN: I certainly wasn't looking at your mother then.

FRANCES: You were thinking about her. Otherwise, you would have never let me say good night so easily.

FRANCES (to JOHN): So this is where you live. Oh, Mother will love it up here!

The Trouble With Harry

CAPT. ALBERT WILES [Edmund Gwenn]: Mother always said I'd come to a bad end.

Psycho

MARION CRANE [Janet Leigh]: We can have dinner—but respectably—in my house, with my mother's picture on the mantel.

SAM LOOMIS [John Gavin]: And after the steak, do we send sister to the movies? Turn Mama's picture to the wall?

CAROLINE [Patricia Hitchcock]: I've got something—not aspirin. My mother's doctor gave them to me the day of my wedding.

MARION: There any calls?

CAROLINE: Teddy called me—My mother called to see if Teddy called.

MARION: Is your time so empty?
NORMAN BATES [Anthony Perkins]: No. Uh—well, I—run the office, and uh—tend the cabins and grounds—do little, uh—errands for my mother—the ones she allows I might be capable of doing.

NORMAN: Well, a son is a poor substitute for a lover.

She's as harmless as one of those stuffed birds.

She just goes a little mad sometimes. We all go a little mad sometimes. Haven't you?

She might have fooled me, but she didn't fool my mother.

DR. RICHMOND [Simon Oakland]: I got the whole story but not from Norman. I got it from his mother. Norman Bates no longer exists.

The Birds

ANNIE HAYWORTH [Suzanne Pleshette] (*referring to* LYDIA BRENNER [Jessica Tandy], *the mother of her former lover,* MITCH BRENNER [Rod Taylor]): When I got back to San Francisco, I spent days trying to figure out exactly what I had done to displease her.
MELANIE DANIELS [Tippi Hedren]: What had you done?
ANNIE: Nothing. I simply existed. So, what's the answer? Jealous woman, right? Clinging, possessive mother. Wrong. With all due respect to Oedipus, I don't think that was the case.
MELANIE: Then what was it?
ANNIE: Lydia liked me. That's the strange part. Now that I'm no longer a threat, we're very good friends.
MELANIE: Why did she object to you?
ANNIE: 'Cause she was afraid.
MELANIE: Afraid you'd take Mitch?

ANNIE: Afraid I'd give Mitch.

MELANIE: I don't understand.

ANNIE: Afraid of any women who would give Mitch the one thing Lydia can't give him—love.

MITCH: You need a mother's care, my child.

MELANIE: Not my mother.

MITCH: Oh, I'm sorry.

MELANIE: What do you have to be sorry about? My mother— don't waste your time. She ditched us when I was eleven and ran off with some hotel man in the East. You know what a mother's love is?

MITCH: Yes, I do.

MELANIE: You mean it's better to be ditched?

MITCH: No, it's better to be loved. Don't you ever see her?

MELANIE: I don't know where she is.

ANNIE (*referring to* LYDIA): You see, she is not afraid of losing Mitch. She is only afraid of being abandoned.

MELANIE: Someone ought to tell her she'd be gaining a daughter.

Shadow of a Doubt

CHARLIE NEWTON [Teresa Wright]: Mother and her gloves. She's always losing things.

JACK GRAHAM [Macdonald Carey]: One day she'll be losing you.

CHARLIE: Mothers don't lose daughters, don't you remember? They gain sons.

Marnie

MARNIE EDGAR [Tippi Hedren]: Why don't you love me, Mama? I've always wondered why you don't.

MARNIE: What are you thinking now, Mama? About the things I've done? What do you think they are? Things that aren't decent, is that it? Well, you think I'm Mr. Pendleton's girl. Is that why you don't want me to touch you? Is that how you think I get the money to set you up?

MARNIE (*to* MARK RUTLAND [Sean Connery]): If you tell my mother about me, I'll kill you.

COUSIN BOB [Bob Sweeney] (*referring to* MARK): All that money spent to celebrate what? That meager, furtive little wedding. He didn't even ask Mother.

LIL MAINWARING [Diane Baker]: I always thought that a girl's best friend was her mother.

Psycho
NORMAN BATES [Anthony Perkins]: A boy's best friend is his mother.

4

Shadow of a Man

Almost each time Alfred Hitchcock was interviewed, he mentioned an event that not only traumatized him but also had a direct influence on his work:

> When I was a very young child—oh, about four years old—my father sent me to the police station with a note. I assume I was being punished. The police locked me in a cell for about five minutes, saying, "This is what we do to naughty boys." And I've been literally terrified of policemen ever since.

This unpleasant childhood experience had an important impact on Hitchcock, even to the point where the director once said he wanted this quote on his tombstone: "You can see what can happen to you if you are not a good boy!" In his films, his male characters were often wrongly accused of a crime and had to prove their innocence. The director might have been trying to exorcise the fact that he felt he had been unjustifiably punished as a child. Hitchcock's men were mostly anti-heroes, troubled, mysterious, and confused. "My hero is always the average man to whom bizarre things happen, rather than vice versa," Hitchcock said. His definition of what a leading male character should be was simple: "Get an ordinary man into an extraordinary situation and keep him there. But it should be done with humor."

This chapter is divided into three distinctive parts: the wrong men, men and women, and a third segment that presents in general terms and in the male characters' own words, the definition of the Hitchcockian male.

"I would put it this way: I don't like to leave anything to chance," Hitchcock used to say. "I don't like the unexpected. I prefer the familiar, and that is why, even when I'm traveling, I always go back to the same hotel and request the same room I stayed in before. It's very important to me to have a clear horizon in front of me whenever possible." While there is probably a little bit of Hitchcock's own personality in all of his leading men, there is no doubt that they are the expression of the kind of man Hitchcock wished he had been.

The Wrong Men

The Lodger (*title card*)
JOE BETTS [Malcolm Keen], a police detective (*referring to the* LODGER [Ivor Novello]): My God, he is innocent! The real Avenger was taken red-handed ten minutes ago.

The 39 Steps
RICHARD HANNAY [Robert Donat]: I know what it is to feel lonely and helpless and to have the whole world against me, and those are things that no men or women ought to feel.

HANNAY (*to* PAMELA [Madeleine Carroll]): Can't you realize the only way to clear myself is to expose these spies?

Young and Innocent
ERICA BURGOYNE [Nova Pilbeam] (*to* ROBERT TISDALL [Derrick de Marney], *who's been accused of murder*): Don't you know what it means if you're caught?
ROBERT: I'll make a rough guess...Horribly rough.
ERICA: Well, it isn't funny, is it?

ROBERT: No, but I can laugh because I'm innocent. You don't believe me, do you? I wish you did.

ROBERT TISDALL (*to* ERICA): If it's any consolation, I want you to know that I'm innocent.

Rebecca

SHE [Joan Fontaine] (*referring to* REBECCA's *death*): But you didn't kill her. It was an accident.

MAXIM DE WINTER [Laurence Olivier]: Who would believe me?

Suspicion

LINA MCLAIDLAW [Joan Fontaine], who suspects her husband of murdering his best friend: Then you didn't go to Paris.

JOHNNY AYSGARTH [Cary Grant]: Of course not. Do you think I would have let some idiot give poor old Beaky that brandy if I had?

Saboteur

BARRY KANE [Robert Cummings] (*to* PAT MARTIN [Priscilla Lane], *referring to the sabotage of a factory*): Don't you believe me? Do you think I had anything to do with this?

CHARLES TOBIN [Otto Kruger] (*referring to* BARRY): He is noble and fine and pure. So he pays the penalty that the noble and the pure must pay in this world. He is misjudged by everyone. Even the police have a completely erroneous impression of him.

Spellbound

JOHN BALLANTYNE [Gregory Peck], who is accused of killing his therapist: I'm someone else. I don't know who.

Strangers on a Train

ANN MORTON [Ruth Roman]: Why didn't you call the police?

GUY HAINES [Farley Granger], who is suspected of his wife's murder when in fact he knows who the real killer is: And have them say what you did. Mr. Haines, how did you get him to do it? And Bruno would say we planned it together.

Frenzy

BABS MILLIGAN [Anna Massey] (*referring to the police*): Well, there's one thing you can do. Go and see them. Tell them what happened, like you told me.

RICHARD BLANEY [Jon Finch], who is suspected of murder: No, I can't do that.

BABS: You got to.

RICHARD: They'd never believe me!

BABS: Why not? I did.

RICHARD: You're not the law. I'm probably the only suspect they've got.

I Confess

FATHER MICHAEL LOGAN [Montgomery Clift], who's been accused of murder: I'm not capable of murder.

To Catch a Thief

FRANCES STEVENS [Grace Kelly]: These robberies all bare your mark, but you claim you're innocent.

JOHN ROBIE [Cary Grant]: I do more than claim. I insist.

JOHN: You don't have to spend every day of your life proving your honesty, but I do.

The Wrong Man

CHRISTOPHER (MANNY) BALESTRERO [Henry Fonda]: I'm completely innocent.

Am I being accused or something? Who says I'm a holdup man or look like one, and what holdup are you talking about? Don't I have a right to know?

Don't you see I'm just trying to tell the truth?

I got arrested for something I didn't do.

MANNY (*to his son*): I hope you never have to go through anything like I did. If you ever do, I hope you got a son just like mine to come back to.

LIEUTENANT BOWERS [Harold J. Stone] (*to* MANNY): It's purely a routine matter. But I'll tell you something. It's nothing for an innocent man to worry about. It's the fellow that's done something wrong that has to worry.

BOWERS: An innocent man has nothing to fear, remember that.

MANNY: They know I'm not guilty. They caught the man who did it. They know I'm innocent.

North by Northwest
ROGER O. THORNHILL [Cary Grant], who is mistaken for another man: I told you I'm not Kaplan, whoever he is!

Frenzy
RICHARD BLANEY [Jon Finch]: But I ask you, in all conscience, is it likely that I would murder a woman I've been married to for ten years?
BABS MILLIGAN [Anna Massey]: If it was true, it would be horrible.
BLANEY: And rape her after ten years of marriage? Violently rape her?
　　And later:
BLANEY: Babs, I swear I'm telling the truth. Do I look like a sex murderer to you? Can you imagine me creeping around London strangling all these women with ties? That's ridiculous. For a start, I only own two.

Men and Women

The Lodger (title card)
JOE BETTS [Malcolm Keen]: I'm keen on golden curls myself.

Murder!
SIR JOHN MENIER [Herbert Marshall] (*to* DIANA BARING [Norah Baring], *who he proved was innocent of murder*): Now, my dear, you must save those tears. They'll be very useful in my new play.

The 39 Steps
RICHARD HANNAY [Robert Donat] (*to* PAMELA [Madeleine Carroll], *referring to the fact that they're handcuffed to one another*): There are twenty million women in this island and I get to be chained to you!

RICHARD (*to* PAMELA): May I ask what earthquake caused your brain to work at last?

Secret Agent
RICHARD ASHENDEN [John Gielgud]: This girl has been issued to me as part of my disguise. She is nothing to me, and I'm nothing to her.

Sabotage
SUPERINTENDENT TALBOT [Matthew Boulton]: Well, what luck with Mrs. Verloc?
TED SPENSER, a detective [John Loder]: She knows nothing, sir. Nothing at all.
TALBOT: What makes you think so?
TED: She has a straight answer to everything, besides her manner.
TALBOT: Pretty woman?
TED: What's that got to do with it, sir?

TALBOT: I know. I'm not too tender hearted myself, especially when women are concerned.

TED (*to* MRS. VERLOC [Sylvia Sidney]): There is a mystery about me, and come to think of it, there is a mystery about most people. Haven't you got some terrible secret?

Young and Innocent
ROBERT TISDALL [Derrick de Marney] (*to* ERICA BURGOYNE [Nova Pilbeam]): That's what I like about you. You're different.

The Lady Vanishes
GILBERT REDMAN [Michael Redgrave] (*to* IRIS HENDERSON [Margaret Lockwood]): Do you know why you fascinate me? I'll tell you. You have two great qualities I used to admire in my father. You haven't any manners at all, and you're always seeing things.

Rebecca
MRS. VAN HOPPER [Florence Bates]: Most girls would give their eyes for a chance to see Monte.
MAXIM DE WINTER [Laurence Olivier]: Wouldn't that rather defeat the purpose?

MAX (*to* SHE [Joan Fontaine]): Please promise me never to wear black satin or pearls or to be thirty six years old.

MAXIM (*to* SHE): It's a pity you have to grow up.

SHE (*referring to her coat*): Do I have to put it on?
MAXIM: Yes, certainly, certainly, certainly. Can't be too careful with children.

JACK FAVELL [George Sanders] (*referring to She*): We must be careful not to shock Cinderella.

GILES LACEY [Nigel Bruce] (*referring to* MRS. DANVERS [Judith Anderson]): You mean she scares you? She's not exactly an oil painting, is she?

MAXIM (referring to Rebecca): She was incapable of love or tenderness or decency.

MAXIM (*referring to* REBECCA): Perhaps I'm mad. It wouldn't make for sanity, would it, living with the devil.

MAXIM (*to* SHE): You thought I loved Rebecca? I hated her!

MAXIM (*to* SHE): It's gone forever, that funny, young, lost look I loved. Won't ever come back. I killed that when I told you about Rebecca. In a few hours you've grown so much older.

FRANK CROWLEY [Melville Cooper] (*referring to* REBECCA): I suppose...I suppose she was the most beautiful creature I ever saw.

MAXIM: What have you been doing with yourself?
SHE: Oh, I've been thinking.
MAXIM: Oh? Why would you want to do that for?

The Paradine Case
ANTHONY KEANE [Gregory Peck] (*to his wife,* GAY [Ann Todd]): I don't know how you came by this unfeminine interest in things.

Mr. and Mrs. Smith
JEFF CUSTER [Gene Raymond] (*to* ANN SMITH [Carole Lombard]): You know, a woman can't control herself entirely by her head, which is probably why we love you.

Suspicion

JOHNNY AYSGARTH [Cary Grant] (*to* LINA MCLAIDLAW [Joan Fontaine]): What does your family call you? Monkey face?

JOHNNY (*to* LINA *after their first kiss*): You're the first woman I've ever met who meant yes when she said yes.

JOHNNY (*referring to his conquests*): One night, when I couldn't fall asleep, I started to count them; you know, the way you count sheep jumping over a fence. I think I passed out on number seventy-three.

Lifeboat

KOVAC [John Hodiak] (*to* CONSTANCE PORTER [Tallulah Bankhead]): You've been all over the world, you've met all kinds of people, but you never write about them, you only write about yourself. You think this whole war is a show put on for you to cover like a Broadway play. And if enough people die before the last act, maybe you might give it four stars.

Spellbound

DR. FLEUROT [John Emery] (*to* CONSTANCE PETERSEN [Ingrid Bergman], *who's has rejected his love*): A woman like you could never get involved with any man, sane or insane.

DR. ALEX BRULOV [Michael Chekhov] (*to* CONSTANCE): Do not complete the sentence with the usual female contradictions. You grant me that I know more than you, but on the other hand, you know more than me. Woman's talk, bah!

The Paradine Case

JUDY FLAQUER [Joan Tetzel] (*referring to* MRS. PARADINE [Valli]): What's she really like?
SIR SIMON FLAQUER [Charles Coburn]: Fascinating, fascinat-

ing. I'm an old ruin, but she certainly brings my pulse up a beat or two.

ANDRE LATOUR [Louis Jourdan] (*referring to* MRS. PARADINE): I wouldn't have served a woman. It's not in my character to do that.
    And later:
LATOUR: I will tell you about Mrs. Paradine. She is bad, bad to the bone. If ever there was an evil woman, she is one.

ANTHONY KEANE [Gregory Peck] (*to his wife,* GAY [Ann Todd]): There you go again, darling, with all your fancy ideas about me.

Rope
BRANDON [John Dall]: Some women are quite charming when they're angry, Janet. Unfortunately, you're not.

RUPERT CADELL [James Stewart]: Mrs. Walker?
JANET WALKER [Joan Chandler]: How did you know?
RUPERT: Brandon has spoken of you.
JANET: Did he do me justice?
RUPERT: Do you deserve justice?

Under Capricorn
CHARLES ADARE [Michael Wilding] (*referring to* LADY HENRIETTA FLUSKY [Ingrid Bergman]): The first work of art I've ever done and it's wonderfully beautiful.

Stage Fright
EVE GILL [Jane Wyman]: Do you think I talk too much?
WILFRID SMITH [Michael Wilding]: No, most women don't talk enough.

WILFRID (*to* EVE): Every time I'm beginning to think I know what color your eyes are, you disappear.

COMMODORE GILL [Alastair Sim] (*addressing a woman who is blackmailing him and his daughter,* EVE): Miss Livingstone, I presume.

NELLIE GOOD [Kay Walsh]: That's not my name.

COMMODORE GILL: No, no. It's Nelly Good, isn't it? But what does a name matter? After all, I could think of lots and lots and lots of more appropriate names for you.

Strangers on a Train

SENATOR MORTON [Leo G. Carroll] (*referring to a murder victim*): She was a human being. Let me remind you that even the most unworthy of us has the right to life in the pursuit of happiness.

Dial M for Murder

TONY WENDICE [Ray Milland] (*referring to his wife,* MARGOT [Grace Kelly]): I suddenly realized how much I'd grown to depend on her.

TONY (*referring to the moment when he realized* MARGOT *might leave him*): I don't remember ever being so scared.

Rear Window

L. B. JEFFRIES [James Stewart] (*referring to* LISA FREEMONT [Grace Kelly], *his girlfriend*): She is too perfect, she is too talented, she is too beautiful, she is too sophisticated, she is too everything but what I want.

STELLA [Thelma Ritter]: Is what you want something you can discuss?

And later:

JEFFRIES: If she only was ordinary. I need a woman who is willing to go anywhere and do anything and love it.

JEFFRIES (*to* LISA): Gee, I'm proud of you!

TOM DOYLE [Wendell Corey], a detective: Look Miss Freemont, that feminine-intuition stuff sells magazines, but in real life it's still a fairy tale. I don't know how many wasted years I've spent tracking down leads based on female intuition.

North by Northwest
LEONARD [Martin Landau] (*to his accomplice*, PHILIP VANDAMM [James Mason]): Call it my woman's intuition if you will, but I've never trusted neatness. Neatness is always the result of deliberate planning.

James Stewart, Grace Kelly, and Alfred Hitchcock on the set of *Rear Window*.

"When you work with Hitch, you don't try to do a scene in two ways. You do it one way. His."   —James Stewart.

"I can't tell you what a welcome sight this is. No wonder your husband still loves you."

James Stewart is referring here to the hearty breakfast Thelma Ritter cooked for him while peeping on his neighbors in *Rear Window*.

Vertigo

JOHN "SCOTTIE" FERGUSON [James Stewart] (*to* JUDY BARTON [Kim Novak]): One doesn't often get a second chance. I want to stop being haunted. You're my second chance, Judy. You're my second chance.

The necklace. That was the slip. I remembered the necklace.

To Catch a Thief

JOHN ROBIE [Cary Grant] (*talking to* DANIELLE FOUSSARD [Brigitte Auber] *and referring to* FRANCES STEVENS [Grace Kelly]): You are just a child, and she is a woman.

JOHN (*to* FRANCES): You're an insecure, pampered woman accustomed to attracting men, but you're not quite sure if they're attracted to you or to your money. You may never know.

Tell me, have you ever been on the psychiatrist's couch?

You're like an American character in an English movie.

JOHN: What you need is something that I have neither the time nor the inclination to give you.
FRANCES: Oh? What is that?
JOHN: Two weeks with a good man in Niagara Falls.

The Trouble With Harry

SAM MARLOWE [John Forsythe] (*referring to* MISS GRAVELEY [Mildred Natwick]): Do you realize that you'll be the first man to cross her threshold?
CAPT. ALBERT WILES [Edmund Gwenn]: She is a well-preserved woman.
SAM: I envy you.
WILES: Yes, very well preserved, and preserves have to be opened someday.

MISS GRAVELEY: How old do you think I am, young man?
SAM: Fifty. How old do you think you are?
MISS GRAVELEY: Forty-two. I could show you my birth certificate.
SAM: I'm afraid you're gonna have to show more than your birth certificate to convince a man of that.

North by Northwest
ROGER O. THORNHILL [Cary Grant]: How does a girl like you get to be a girl like you?
EVE KENDALL [Eva Marie Saint]: Lucky, I guess.
ROGER: No, not lucky. Naughty, wicked, up to no good.

ROGER (*to* EVE): You're the smartest girl I ever spent the night with on the train.

The PROFESSOR [Leo G. Carroll] (*referring to* EVE): If I thought there was any chance of changing your mind, I'd talk about Miss Kendall, of whom you so obviously disapprove.
ROGER: Yes, for using sex like some people use a fly swatter.

ROGER: Oh, you're that type.
EVE: What type?
ROGER: Honest.
EVE: Not really.
ROGER: Good, because honest women frighten me.
EVE: Why?
ROGER: I don't know. Somehow they seem to put me into disadvantage.
EVE: Because you're not honest with them.
ROGER: Exactly.

Suspicion
JOHNNY AYSGARTH [Cary Grant] (*to* LINA MCLAIDLAW [Joan Fontaine]): I'm honest because with you I think it's the best way to get results.

JOHNNY (*to* LINA): I think I'm falling in love with you, and I don't quite like it. That's why I stayed away from you for one week. I was afraid of you.

Notorious
DEVLIN [Cary Grant]: I've always been scared of women, but I get over it.

Marnie
SIDNEY STRUTT [Martin Gabel] (*referring to* MARNIE [Tippi Hedren]): Certainly I can describe her. Five feet five. One hundred and ten pounds. Size-eight dress. Blue eyes. Black wavy hair. Even features. Good teeth.

STRUTT (*referring to* MARNIE): The little witch. I'll have her put away for twenty years. I knew she was too good to be true. Always so eager to work overtime, never made a mistake, always pulling her skirt down over her knees as though they were a national treasure. She seemed so nice, so efficient, so...
MARK RUTLAND [Sean Connery]: Resourceful?

MARNIE: Does zoology include people, Mr. Rutland?
MARK: Well, in a way it includes all the animal ancestors from whom man derives his instincts.
MARNIE: Ladies' instincts, too?
MARK: Well, that paper deals with the instincts of predators. What you might call the criminal class of the animal world. Lady animals figure very largely as predators.

MARK (*to* MARNIE): You know, I wouldn't have pegged you for a woman who was afraid of anything.

We've established that you're a thief and a liar. Now, what is the degree? Are you a compulsive thief? A pathological liar?

You're unquestionably the best-looking woman here, the best dressed, the most intelligent, and you're with me.

Dad goes by scent. If he smells anything like a horse, you're in.

Frenzy
INSPECTOR OXFORD [Alec McCowen]: These days, ladies abandon their honor far more readily than their clothes.

Family Plot
GEORGE LUMLEY [Bruce Dern] (*to his girlfriend*, BLANCHE TYLER [Barbara Harris]): I'm sick and tired of having you have me by the crystal balls.

More About Men

The Lodger (title card)
JOE BETTS [Malcolm Keen] (*referring to the* LODGER [Ivor Novello]): Anyway, I'm glad he's not keen on girls.

Secret Agent
RICHARD ASHENDEN [John Gielgud]: As soon as I landed in England, I found out that I was dead!

The Lady Vanishes
GILBERT REDMAN [Michael Redgrave]: I'm just about as popular as a dose of strychnine.

Rebecca
MAXIM DE WINTER [Laurence Olivier] (*to* SHE [Joan Fontaine]): If you say we're happy, let's leave it at that. Happiness is something I know nothing about.

JACK FAVELL [George Sanders]: You've known Max a long

time, so you know he is the old-fashioned type who'd die to defend his honor or who'd kill for it.

Foreign Correspondent

JOHNNY JONES [Joel McCrea]: I'm just as big a jackass as I ever was. Bigger.

Listen, Mr. Fisher, I've covered beer mob killings and race riots since I was a tot without carrying a rabbit's foot.

If anyone finds out I've hired a bodyguard, I'll shoot myself.

Suspicion

JOHNNY AYSGARTH [Cary Grant]: To tell you the truth, I'm a little bored with people in my alley!

JOHNNY (*to* LINA MCLAIDLAW [Joan Fontaine]): Monkey face, I've always had the notion that the secret of success is to start at the top.

People don't change overnight. I'm no good.

The Paradine Case

LORD HORFIELD [Charles Laughton]: Please, Sir Simon, I don't like to be interrupted in the middle of an insult.

Rope

BRANDON [John Dall] (*referring to* RUPERT CADELL [James Stewart]): Rupert is extremely radical. Do you know that he selects his books on the assumption that people not only can read but actually can think. Curious fellow, but I like him.

RUPERT: You know, Philip, I get quite intrigued when people don't answer questions, and quite curious.

Strangers on a Train
GUY HAINES [Farley Granger]: It's kinda painful for a man to discover he's been a chump.

I Confess
FATHER MICHAEL LOGAN [Montgomery Clift]: I don't hate anyone, Keller.

Rear Window
A VOICE on the radio: Men, are you over forty? When you wake up in the morning, do you feel tired and run-down? Do you have that restless feeling?

L.B. JEFFRIES [James Stewart]: I'm not stubborn; I'm truthful.

JEFFRIES: Right now, I'd welcome trouble.

Sabotage
TED SPENSER [John Loder]: I like trouble.

To Catch a Thief
FRANCES STEVENS [Grace Kelly]: John, why bother?
JOHN ROBIE [Cary Grant]: Sort of a hobby of mine: the truth.

Vertigo
JOHN "SCOTTIE" FERGUSON [James Stewart]: I have agoraphobia, which gives me vertigo.

I look up, I look down.

I'm a man of independent means, as the saying goes. Fairly independent.

JOHN, who broke his ribs during a chase that left him hanging

"One doesn't often get a second chance. I want to stop being haunted."

James Stewart gets dizzy from Kim Novak in *Vertigo*.

from a rooftop: Tomorrow the corset comes off. Tomorrow I'll be able to scratch myself like anybody else.

Rear Window
JEFFRIES [James Stewart], who broke one leg while taking pictures of a race-car crash: Next Wednesday I emerge from that plaster cocoon.

Topaz
ANDRE DEVEREAUX [Frederick Stafford]: And I'm supposed to keep my mouth shut and uncover Topaz at the risk of my own skin? That's quite a job, my friends.

5

Psychos, Murder, and Death

Villains

An Agatha Christie–type character in *Suspicion* says about the villains in her mystery novels: "I always think of my murderers as my heroes." This quote parallels Hitchcock's own treatment of the bad guys in his films:

> I always make my villains charming and polite. It's a mistake to think that if you put a villain on the screen, he must sneer nastily, stroke his black mustache, or kick a dog in the stomach. Some of the most famous murderers in criminology—men for whom arsenic was so disgustingly gentle that they did women in with blunt instruments—had to be charmers to get acquainted with the females they murdered. The really frightening thing about villains is their surface likableness.

Hitchcock was a master at making his killers almost as appealing to the audience as his real heroes. First of all, they have a cynical sense of humor, and though their view of the world is sinister, it seems amusing. Of course, the fact that they take this one step further and act on it by doing away with a few human beings whom they consider inferior is the frightening part. However, by the time we realize that, Hitchcock has already tricked us into liking his villains. "The

murderer in *Frenzy*," Hitchcock said, "is a very cheerful
fellow. Most people make murderers so sinister, they'd never
get near a girl." While looks are deceiving, words are not, and
it's the ambiguous dialogue spoken by or about Hitchcock's
bad guys that betrays them and reveals their true evil nature.

Murder!

HANDEL FANE [Esme Percy] (*a transvestite and also a killer*): I
assure you, Inspector, I'm not the other woman in the case!

DIANA BARING [Norah Baring] (*referring to* HANDEL
FANE): Why, the man's half-caste!

The 39 Steps

ANNABELLA SMITH [Lucie Mannheim] (*referring to* PROFESSOR
JORDAN [Godfrey Tearle], *a spy*): He has a dozen names. He
can look like a hundred people. But one thing he can't
disguise. This part of his little finger is missing. So if ever you
should meet a man with no top joint there, be very careful, my
friend.

PROFESSOR JORDAN: You see, I live here as a respectable
citizen, and you must realize that my whole existence would
be jeopardized if it became known that I'm not—what should
we say?—not what I seem.

RICHARD HANNAY [Robert Donat]: All the information is
inside Memory's head!

HANNAY: What are the thirty-nine steps?
MR. MEMORY [Wylie Watson], a man who's been passing
secrets to a spy ring): The thirty-nine steps is an organization
of spies collecting information on the behalf of the foreign
office.

Sabotage

STEVIE [Desmond Tester] (*referring to* TED SPENSER [John Loder] *a detective*): He says gangsters are not nearly as frightening as you'd think. Some of them are quite ordinary looking, like you and me and Mr. Verloc. Perhaps he's right. After all, if gangsters looked like gangsters, the police would soon get after them, wouldn't they?

Jamaica Inn

SIR HUMPHREY PENGALLAN [Charles Laughton]: You're not as good as I am; you never will be.

SIR HUMPHREY (before jumping to death): I shall be down to you before you're up to me, Mr. Traherne.

Foreign Correspondent

STEPHEN FISHER [Herbert Marshall], before giving himself in: It's time for me to make a landing. A forced one.

Saboteur

FREEMAN [Alan Baxter] an accomplice of CHARLES TOBIN's [Otto Kruger], a saboteur and traitor: Yes, that's one of the things I like about old Tobin, his love for that little girl. Evidence of a good heart. I have children, too, you know.
BARRY KANE [Robert Cummings]: Oh?
FREEMAN: Two boys. Nice little fellows. Age two and four. The four-year-old is naughty at times; he is quite a problem. We give him a new toy, and within half an hour it's smashed to bits, and then, sometimes, after it's all over, he seems almost sorry. Sometimes I wish my younger child had been a girl. In fact, my wife and I often argue about a little idiosyncrasy I have. I don't want his hair cut short until he is much older. Do you think it will be bad for him?
BARRY: Well, I don't know. It might.

FREEMAN: When I was a child, I had long golden curls. People used to stop on the street to admire me.
BARRY: Things are different nowadays. If you give a kid a haircut, it might save him a lot of grief.

TOBIN (*to* BARRY): Power. Yes, I want that as much as you want your comfort, your job, or that girl. We all have different tastes, as you can see, only I'm willing to back my tastes with the necessary force.

Shadow of a Doubt
UNCLE CHARLIE OAKLEY [Joseph Cotten], also known as "The Merry Widow Murderer": Everybody was sweet and pretty then, Charlie. The whole world. Wonderful world. Not like the world today. Not like the world now. It was great to be young then.

I've never been photographed, and I don't want to be.

It's not good to find out too much, Charlie.

What's the use of looking backward? What's the use of looking ahead? Today is the thing. That's my philosophy. Today.

The whole world is a joke to me.

I guess heaven takes care of fools and scoundrels.

Ah, details. I'm glad to see that you're a man who understands details, Mr. Green. They're most important to me. Most important. All the little details.

I like people who face facts.

(*referring to Sunday mass*): The show has been running for such a long time, I thought attendance might be falling off.

CHARLIE NEWTON [Teresa Wright] (*referring to a picture of her uncle* CHARLIE *as a child*): Uncle Charlie, you were beautiful.
EMMA NEWTON [Patricia Collinge], CHARLIE's mother and UNCLE CHARLIE's sister: Wasn't he, though? And such a quiet boy, always reading. I always said Papa should never have bought you that bicycle; you didn't know how to handle it. Charlie, he took it right out on the icy road and skid it into a streetcar. We thought he was going to die.
CHARLIE: I'm glad he didn't.
EMMA: Well, he almost did. He fractured his skull. And he was laid up for so long, and then, when he was getting well, there was no holding him. It was just as though all the rest he had was, well, too much for him and he had to get into mischiefs to blow up steam. He didn't do much reading after that, let me tell you.

UNCLE CHARLIE: Women keep me busy in towns like this. In the cities, it's different. The cities are full of women, middle-aged, widows, husbands dead. Husbands who spent their lives making fortunes, working and working. Then they die and leave the money to their wives, their silly wives. What do the wives do, these useless women? You see them in the hotels, the best hotels, every day by the thousands, drinking the money, eating the money, losing the money at bridge, playing all day and all night, smelling of money. Proud of their jewelry but of nothing else. Horrible...Faded, fat, greedy women.
CHARLIE, his niece [Teresa Wright]: But they're alive, they're human beings.
UNCLE CHARLIE: Are they? Are they, Charlie? Are they human, or are they fat, wheezing [sic] animals, uh? What happens to animals when they get too fat and too old?

UNCLE CHARLIE (*to his niece,* CHARLIE): You're just an ordinary little girl, living in an ordinary little town. You wake up every morning of your life, you know perfectly well there is nothing to trouble you. You go through your ordinary little day, and at night you sleep your untroubled, ordinary little sleep filled with peaceful, stupid dreams. But I brought you nightmares.

UNCLE CHARLIE (*to* CHARLIE): Do you know the world is a foul stye? Do you know if you ripped the front off houses, you'd find swine? The world is a hell. What does it matter what happens in it?

CHARLIE NEWTON: I hope Mr. Saunders does not move anything there. My uncle is awfully neat and fussy.

CHARLIE NEWTON (*referring to her uncle*): He thought the world was a horrible place. He didn't trust people. He seemed to hate them. He hated the whole world. You know, he said that people like us had no idea what the world was really like.

JACK GRAHAM [Macdonald Carey]: It's not quite as bad as that, but sometimes it needs a lot of watching. Seems to go crazy every now and then, like your uncle Charlie.

Notorious
ALEXANDER SEBASTIAN [Claude Rains] (*referring to* ERIC MATHIS [Ivan Triesault], *a killer*): You know, Eric loves to go to the movies to cry. He's very sentimental.

SEBASTIAN: I'm not afraid to die.

ERIC (*Who realizes* ALEX SEBASTIAN *has betrayed his confidence*): Alex, will you come in, please. I wish to talk to you.

Rope
BRANDON [John Dall] (*to his lover,* PHILIP [Farley Granger], *after committing a murder*): It's the darkness that got you down. Nobody ever feels really safe in the dark. Nobody who was ever a child, that is.

PHILIP (*to* BRANDON): You frighten me. You always have. From the very first day in prep school. Part of your charms, I suppose.

BRANDON: Being weak is a mistake.
PHILIP: Because it's being human?
BRANDON: Because it's being ordinary.

MRS. ATWATER [Constance Collier] (*to* PHILIP, *a pianist but also a strangler*): These hands will bring you great fame.

RUPERT CADELL [James Stewart] (*to* BRANDON): You always did stutter when you got excited.

BRANDON: Good and evil, right and wrong, were invented for the ordinary, average man, the inferior man, because he needs them.

Strangers on a Train
BRUNO ANTHONY [Robert Walker]: I certainly admire people who do things.

People who do things are important. Me, I never seem to do anything.

I have a theory that you should do everything before you die.

North by Northwest
ROGER O. THORNHILL [Cary Grant] (*to* PHILIP VANDAMM [James Mason], *a traitor;* LEONARD [Martin Landau], *his accomplice;* and EVE KENDALL [Eva Marie Saint], *a double agent*): The three of you together. Now, that's a picture only Charles Addams could draw.

The PROFESSOR [Leo G. Carroll] (*referring to* VANDAMM): He is a sort of importer/exporter.

ROGER O. THORNHILL [Cary Grant]: Of what?
The PROFESSOR: Oh, government secrets.

VANDAMM (*to* LEONARD *and referring to* EVE): You know what I think? I think you're jealous. No, I mean it. I'm very touched, very.

Psycho
NORMAN BATES [Anthony Perkins]: I think I must have one of those faces you just can't help believing.

I'm not capable of being fooled! Not even by a woman.

MILTON ARBOGAST, a private detective [Martin Balsam]: Would you mind looking at the picture before committing yourself?
NORMAN: Commit myself? You sure talk like a policeman.

Frenzy
BOB RUSK [Barry Foster], a dangerous killer: People like me. I've got things to give.

INSPECTOR OXFORD [Alec McCowen] (*to* BOB RUSK, *the necktie murderer*): Mr. Rusk, you're not wearing your tie.

A MAN [Noel Johnson] discusses the necktie murderer in an English pub: On the surface, in casual conversation, they appear as ordinary, likable, adult fellows, but emotionally they remain as dangerous children whose conduct may revert to a primitive, subhuman level at any moment.

Family Plot
ARTHUR ADAMSON [William Devane] (*to* FRAN [Karen Black], *his accomplice and girlfriend*): I told you about danger, didn't I? At first, it makes you sick, and when you get through with it, it makes you very, very loving.

Murder and Death

"People ask me constantly," Hitchcock once said, "'Why are you so interested in crime?' The truth is I'm not. I'm only interested in it as it affects my profession." At the same time, the director, who was born in England and lived there a good part of his life, acknowledged that crime had always been an English passion. Visually, Hitchcock filmed murders with style; his dialogue treated killings with equal reverence and respect. "Crime must be stylish," the director said. "It must have imagination and originality. I believe, furthermore, that logic is dull. I approach crime with fantasy." Whether he knew it or denied it to himself, Hitchcock was fascinated with crime and approached murder and death in his movies as he did love and marriage: with great cynicism and humor. Maybe to him they were all one and the same thing.

The Lodger (title card)
A FEMALE MODEL: He's killed another fair girl. No more peroxide for yours truly.

Blackmail
A CUSTOMER [Phyllis Monkman] to the owners of a tobacco shop: Whatever the provocation, I could never use a knife.

MR. WHITE [Charles Paton] (to ALICE WHITE [Anny Ondra], who has murdered a rapist with a knife and referring to the knife she has dropped on the floor): You know, you should have been more careful. Might have cut somebody with that.

The Man Who Knew Too Much (1934)
ABBOTT [Peter Lorre] (giving instructions to his hired killer): If you listen, my dear Ramón, I'll show the exact moment at which you shoot. Now listen carefully... There, you see, such a moment, your shot will not be heard. I think the composer would have appreciated that. No one will know.

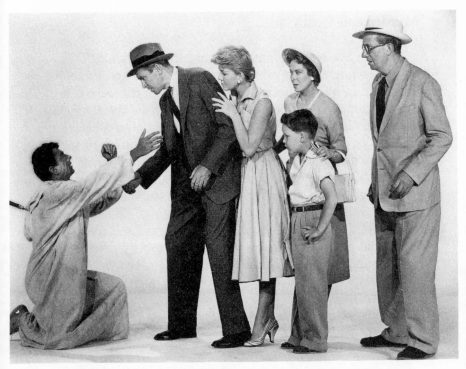

"A man, a statesman is to be killed, assassinated in London. Soon, very soon."

From left: Daniel Gélin, James Stewart, Doris Day, Christopher Olsen, Brenda de Banzie, and Bernard Miles in *The Man Who Knew Too Much.*

RAMON LEVINE [Frank Vosper]: Except for one.
ABBOTT: If you're clever, my friend. Come, you must start soon. It's impolite to be late for a concert.

The same scene in the remake of *The Man Who Knew Too Much* (1956):
MR. DRAYTON [Bernard Miles]: Now, if you listen, I'm going to play you the exact moment at which you can shoot. So listen carefully...Now, once more...Listen for the crash of the

cymbals... You see, at such a moment, your shot will never be heard. Even the listeners will be undisturbed. I think the composer would have appreciated it, don't you? No one will know.

RIEN [Reggie Nalder]: No one except one.

MR. DRAYTON: That's right, if you're clever, my friend.

Secret Agent

RICHARD ASHENDEN [John Gielgud] (*to* ELSA CARRINGTON [Madeleine Carroll]): It's murder and you call it fun!

ELSA (*referring to a killing*): You mean we may have to—How thrilling!

Young and Innocent

GUY [George Curzon]: What did I do with the belt? I twisted it around her neck and choked the life out of her.

The Lady Vanishes

DR. HARTZ [Paul Lukas] (*referring to* MISS FROY [Dame May Whitty] whom he intends to murder): She will be removed from the hospital there and operated on. Unfortunately, the operation will not be successful. Oh, I should perhaps have explained. The operation will be performed by me.

Rebecca

MAXIM DE WINTER [Laurence Olivier]: I knew where Rebecca's body was, lying on that cabin floor at the bottom of the sea.

SHE [Joan Fontaine]: How did you know, Max?

MAXIM: Because, I put it there.

Suspicion

BEAKY THWAITE [Nigel Bruce] (*playing Scrabble*): If I had an "e-r," I could make that MURDERER.

ISOBEL SEDBUSK [Auriol Lee], a mystery novelist: I always think of my murderers as my heroes.

JOHNNY AYSGARTH [Cary Grant]: If you're going to kill someone, do it simply.

LINA MCLAIDLAW [Joan Fontaine] (*referring to poison*): Is whatever it is painful?
ISOBEL: Not in the least. In fact, I should think it should be the most pleasant death.

Psycho
A FEMALE CUSTOMER at SAM's [John Gavin] hardware store: They tell you what its ingredients are, and how it's guaranteed to exterminate every insect in the world, but they do not tell you whether or not it's painless. And—and I say, insect or man, death should always be painless.

Shadow of a Doubt
JOE NEWTON [Henry Travers]: The best way to commit a murder—
HERB HAWKINS [Hume Cronyn]: I know, I know. Hit them on the head with a blunt instrument.

CHARLIE NEWTON [Teresa Wright]: What's the matter with you two? Do you always have to talk about killing people?
JOE, her father: We're not talking about killing people. Herb is talking about killing me, and I'm talking about killing him.
EMMA NEWTON [Patricia Collinge], her mother: It's your father's way of relaxing.

The Paradine Case
GAY KEANE [Ann Todd]: Well, nice people don't go murdering other nice people.

ANTHONY KEANE [Gregory Peck], a lawyer on a murder trial: I have a murderous day tomorrow.

Rope

In *Rope*, BRANDON [John Dall] and his lover, PHILIP [Farley Granger], have strangled one of their friends:

BRANDON: The good Americans usually die young on the battlefield, don't they? Well, the Davids of the world merely occupy space, which is why he was the perfect victim for the perfect crime.

Well, murder can be an art, too. The power to kill can be as satisfying as the power to create.

We killed for the sake of danger and for the sake of killing.

Nobody commits murder just for the experience of committing it. Nobody except us.

BRANDON: Murder is a crime for most men...
PHILIP: ...but a privilege for the few.

PHILIP: How did you feel?
BRANDON: When?
PHILIP: During it.
BRANDON: I don't know, really. I don't remember feeling very much of anything until his body went limp and I knew it was all over.
PHILIP: And then?
BRANDON: And then I felt tremendously exhilarated.

RUPERT CADELL [James Stewart] (*jokingly approving of murder*): Think of the problems it would solve: unemployment, poverty, standing in line for theater tickets.

Now mind you, I don't hold with the extremists who feel there should be open season for murder all year around. No, personally I would prefer to have Cut a Throat Week, Strangulation Day.

Knives may not be used on hotel employees. They are in the death-by-slow-torture category, along with bird lovers, small children, and tap dancers.

Unfortunately, RUPERT realizes that BRANDON and PHILIP have taken his words seriously and have applied his theories on murder to real life:

RUPERT: But you've given my words a meaning that I've never dreamed of, and you've tried to twist them into a cold, logical excuse for your ugly murder.

You strangled the life out of a fellow human being who could live and love as you never could and never will again.

Stage Fright

CHARLOTTE INWOOD [Marlene Dietrich] (*referring to her husband*): Johnny, you love me, say that you love me. You do love me, don't you? I think he's dead. I'm sure he's dead. I didn't mean it. I didn't mean it.

The only murderer here is the orchestra leader.

It's the scene of the crime the murderer returns to, not the theater.

EVE GILL [Jane Wyman]: What do you say we go and hear Charlotte sing?

CHUBBY BANNISTER [Patricia Hitchcock]: Oh, do let's. The murder makes her so interesting.

JONATHAN COOPER [Richard Todd] (*to* EVE, *referring to the two murders he's committed*): There is nothing wrong with my mind. Nobody can prove that there is unless...unless I do it a third time with no reason whatever. That would be a clear case of insanity, wouldn't it? Wouldn't it?

Spellbound

DR. MURCHISON [Leo G. Carroll], a killer (*to* CONSTANCE PETERSEN [Ingrid Bergman]): You forget in your imbecilic devotion to your patient that the punishment for two murders is the same as for one.

CONSTANCE PETERSEN (*to* DR. MURCHISON): A man with your intelligence does not commit a stupid murder.

And later:

If you shoot now, it is called deliberate murder. You'll be tried as a sane murderer. Convicted as a sane man and killed in the electric chair for your crimes.

Strangers on a Train

BRUNO ANTHONY [Robert Walker]: Want to hear one of my ideas about the perfect murder? You want to hear the busted light socket in the bathroom or the carbon monoxide in the garage?

Everyone has somebody that they want to put out of the way. Oh, now, surely, madam, you're not going to tell me that there hasn't been a time that you didn't want to dispose of someone. Your husband, for instance.

I have the best way and the best tools. Simple, silent, and quick, the last part being the most important one. Let me show you what I mean. You don't mind if I borrow your neck for a moment, do you?

I have a murder on my conscience. But it's not my murder, Mr. Haines, it's yours, and since you're the one to profit by it, I think you should be the one to pay for it.

GUY HAINES [Farley Granger]: I may be old-fashioned, but I thought murder was against the law.

GUY (*referring to his wife, who refuses to give him a divorce*): Sure, I sound savage. I feel savage. I'd like to break her neck. I said I'd like to break her foul, useless little neck."

BARBARA MORTON [Patricia Hitchcock]: I still think it would be wonderful to have a man love you so much, he'd kill for you.

Guy, did you know Mr. Hennessy helped crack that ax murder I've been reading about? You know, the one with the body that was cut up and hidden in the butcher's shop. He was locked in the icebox with the left leg for six hours.

MRS. CUNNINGHAM [Norma Varden] (*a guest at a party, joking about murder*): I can take him out in the car and, when we get to a very lonely spot, knock him on the head with a hammer, pour gasoline over him and over the car, and set the whole thing ablaze.

SENATOR MORTON [Leo G. Carroll] (*to his daughter,* BARBARA): Young lady, there is no overlooking the fact that murder is at our doorstep, but I wish that you wouldn't drag it into the living room.

I Confess
FATHER MICHAEL LOGAN [Montgomery Clift]: Vilette has been murdered!

RUTH GRANDFORT [Anne Baxter]: He's dead? I can't believe it! We're free!

Dial M for Murder

TONY WENDICE [Ray Milland] (*referring to his wife,* MARGOT [Grace Kelly], *and her boyfriend,* MARK HALLIDAY [Robert Cummings]): I thought of three different ways of killing him. I even thought of killing her. That seemed the far more sensible idea.

LASGATE [Anthony Dawson] (*referring to the police*): I should simply tell them that you're trying to blackmail me into—
WENDICE: Into?
LASGATE: Murdering your wife.

WENDICE: One thousand pounds.
LASGATE: For a murder?
WENDICE: For a few minutes' work. That's all it is.

WENDICE: That's what I should tell the police.
LASGATE (*referring to* WENDICE's *wife*): Yes, but she may say that—
WENDICE: But she isn't going to say anything, is she?

TONY: People don't commit murder on credit.

MARGOT (*to her husband, who has hired a killer to murder her, and boyfriend, who writes murder mysteries*): Why don't you two collaborate? A detective novel with a tennis background.
WENDICE: What about it, Mark? You provide me with the perfect murder.
MARK: Nothing I'd like better.

WENDICE: Do you really believe in the perfect murder?

MARK: Uh? Yes, absolutely. On paper, that is. And I think I could plan one out better than most people, but I doubt that I could carry it out.
WENDICE: Oh, why not?
MARK: Well, because in stories things turn out the way the authors want them to and in real life they don't.

At the end of the film, TONY is caught:
As you said, Mark, it might work on paper.

Rear Window
LISA FREEMONT [Grace Kelly]: Why would Thorwald want to kill a little dog? Because it knew too much!

LISA (*to* L. B. JEFFRIES [James Stewart]: Look at you and me, plunged into despair because we find out a man didn't kill his wife. We're the two most frightening ghouls I've ever known.

STELLA [Thelma Ritter]: A murderer would never parade his crime in front of an open window.

STELLA: You haven't spent much time around cemeteries, have you? Mr. Thorwald could scarcely put his wife's body in a plot of ground of about one foot square. Unless, of course, he put her standing on end; then he wouldn't need a knife and saw. My idea is that she is scattered all over town.

STELLA (*referring to the fact that she doesn't want to see the head of* THORWALD's *wife, which he has hidden in a hat box*): No, thanks, I don't want any part of it.

The Trouble With Harry
MISS GRAVELEY [Mildred Natwick] (*referring to a man's dead body*): What seems to be the trouble, Captain?
CAPT. ALBERT WILES [Edmund Gwenn]: Well, what you might call an unavoidable accident. He's dead.

MISS GRAVELEY: Yes, I'd say that he was. Of course, that's an unprofessional opinion.

CAPTAIN WILES (*while having a cup of coffee*): A real handsome man's cup.

MISS GRAVELEY: It's been in the family for years. My father always used it... until he died.

CAPTAIN WILES: I trust he died peacefully. Slipped away in the night.

MISS GRAVELEY: He was caught in a threshing machine.

SAM MARLOWE [John Forsythe] (*to* CAPTAIN WILES *and referring to the man he believes he shot accidentally*): In a way, you should be grateful that you were able to do your share in accomplishing the destiny of a fellow human being.

SAM (*to the captain*): If you must kill things, I'd wish you'd stick to rabbits. The body is smaller.

JENNIFER ROGERS [Shirley MacLaine] (*referring to her dead husband*): He looked exactly the same when he was alive, only he was vertical.

JENNIFER: Murder is murder, no matter how exonerating the circumstances.

SAM: I'd rather be thought a murderer than proved one.

SAM: If it's murder, who done it?
CAPTAIN WILES: Who did it?
SAM: That's what I said, who done it?

MISS GRAVELEY: I'm grateful to you for burying my body.

JENNIFER: I've never been to a homemade funeral before.
CAPTAIN WILES: I have. This is my third... All in one day.

The Man Who Knew Too Much (1956)

LOUIS BERNARD [Daniel Gélin] (*to* BEN MCKENNA [James Stewart]): A man, a statesman, is to be killed, assassinated in London. Soon, very soon. Tell them in London to try Ambrose Chappell.

Vertigo

JUDY BARTON [Kim Novak] (*in a letter to* JOHN "SCOTTIE" FERGUSON [James Stewart]): You have nothing to blame yourself for. You were the victim. I was the tool, and you were the victim of Gavin Elster's plan to murder his wife.

JOHN (*to* JUDY): You shouldn't keep souvenirs of a killing. You shouldn't have been that sentimental.

North by Northwest

EVE KENDALL [Eva Marie Saint]: How do I know you aren't a murderer?
ROGER O. THORNHILL [Cary Grant]: You don't.
EVE: Maybe you're planning to murder me right here tonight.
ROGER: Shall I?
EVE: Please do.

ROGER (*to* PHILIP VANDAMM [James Mason]): I didn't realize you were an art collector. I thought you only collected corpses.

ROGER: The only performance that will satisfy you is when I play dead.
VANDAMM: Your very next role. You'll be quite convincing, I assure you.

ROGER: I wonder what subtle form of manslaughter is next on the program.

Psycho

CASSIDY [Frank Albertson] (*referring to* MARION CRANE [Janet Leigh] *who has stolen $40,000 from him*): Well, I ain't about to kiss off forty thousand dollars! I'll get it back, and if any of it's missin', I'll replace it with her fine, soft flesh.

The Birds

CATHY BRENNER [Veronica Cartwright] (*referring to one of her brother's* [Rod Taylor] *clients*): He's got a client who shot his wife in the head six times. Six times, can you imagine it? I mean, even twice would be overdoing it, don't you think?

Frenzy

BOB RUSK [Barry Foster] (*before he rapes and kills a woman*): You're my type of woman.

RUSK (*while raping one of his victims*): Lovely! Lovely! Lovely!

RUSK: Bitch! Women! They're all the same. I'll show you.

MAISY [June Ellis], a waitress in a pub: He rapes them first, doesn't he?
CUSTOMER #1 [Noel Johnson]: Yes, I believe he does.
CUSTOMER #2 [Gerald Sim]: Well, I suppose it's nice to know every cloud has a silver lining.

Family Plot

ARTHUR ADAMSON [William Devane] (*to his accomplice* MALONEY [Ed Lauter]): Isn't it touching now? A perfect murder has kept our friendship alive.

6

To Catch a Meal

Food

Hitchcock's greatest preoccupation was not sex, women, or crime. It was food. While it had a place of honor in his everyday life, it quickly became an important theme in his films; food is linked to (or is the substitute for) marriage, sex, and murder. Food is as abundant in his films as it was on his table and was a major item in the Hitchcock family budget. Even in the days when he had no money and lived in England, the director would borrow a pound and spend it on a good meal. Hitchcock brought his own cook to Hollywood when he and his wife moved to America and imported English bacon and Dover soles, which he kept in storage at the Los Angeles Smoking and Curing Co. His favorite restaurant in Hollywood was Dave Chasen's, and when he dined there, he usually ordered a double steak and a champagne punch made according to his own specifications. Hitchcock liked to show the characters in his films eating and thought that movies in color especially brought out the aesthetics of food and drink.

Hitchcock, on food and sex: "I do not believe in raw sex. I like my sex cooked, preferably with a delicate sauce."

Hitchcock, on eggs: "I loathe the living sight of them."

Hitchcock, on food and film: "There will obviously be a lot of drama in the steak that is too rare."

"Cinema is not a slice of life, it's a piece of cake."

The Hitchcock diet plan: "A few years ago, in Santa Rosa, California, I caught a side view of myself in a store window and screamed with fright. Since then, I limit myself to a three-course dinner of appetizer, fish, and meat, with only one bottle of vintage wine with each course."

Food and Marriage

The 39 Steps
THE CROFTER [John Laurie] (*to his wife* [Peggy Ashcroft]): "Is the supper ready, woman?

Sabotage
MRS. JONES [Martita Hunt], the cook: "I've got to hurry home 'cause my husband is having trouble with his kidneys again and I can't leave him alone. Your young brother is looking after them.
RENEE [Joyce Barbour]: What, the kidneys?
MRS. JONES: No, the vegetables.

Mr. and Mrs. Smith
ANN SMITH [Carole Lombard] (*referring to her difficult relationship with her husband*, DAVID [Robert Montgomery]: I used to think maybe it was the things he ate. I tried to change his diet around and everything.

DAVID (*to his wife*): When a man has been sitting across the breakfast table from the same woman for three solid years and still wants to marry her, she is quite a girl.

Shadow of a Doubt

JOE NEWTON [Henry Travers] (*referring to his wife*, EMMA (Patricia Collinge]): I couldn't pursuade her to come to the station. Dinner came first.

Notorious

ALICIA HUBERMAN [Ingrid Bergman] (*to* DEVLIN [Cary Grant]): We're going to have knives and forks, after all. I've decided we're going to eat in style. Marriage must be wonderful with this happening every day.

ALICIA (*referring to* ALEX SEBASTIAN [Claude Rains]: He wants me to marry him, and I have to give him my answer at lunch.

Rear Window

L. B. JEFFRIES [James Stewart] (*to* STELLA [Thelma Ritter], *and referring to the meal she's cooked for him*): I can't tell you what a welcome sight this is. No wonder your husband still loves you.

JEFFRIES: Would you fix me a sandwich, please?
STELLA (*referring to the fact that he should get married*): Yes, I will, and I'll spread a little common sense on the bread.

The Wrong Man

ROSE BALESTRERO [Vera Miles] (*to her husband*, MANNY [Henry Fonda], *as she picks him up at the jail*): Manny, we're going home now. I've got some coffee and lasagna. Manny, you'll be all right.

The Birds

LYDIA BRENNER [Jessica Tandy] (*referring to her deceased husband*): Sometimes, even now, I wake up in the morning, and I think I must get Frank's breakfast. I get up—It's a good reason for getting out of bed, until, of course, I remember.

Torn Curtain

SARAH SHERMAN [Julie Andrews] (*to* MICHAEL ARMSTRONG [Paul Newman], *her fiancé*): You're a scientist and you're supposed to respect the natural order in all things. Breakfast comes before lunch...And marriage should come before a honeymoon cruise.

SARAH: Oh, look, Michael, we could get an apartment. I mean, I could look after you, shop, cook.

Frenzy

INSPECTOR OXFORD [Alec McCowen] (*to his wife* [Vivien Merchant], *who is experimenting with new recipes*): What does your intuition tell you I want for dinner tonight?
MRS. OXFORD: Steak and a baked potato, but you're getting *pied de porc à la mode de Caen*.
INSPECTOR OXFORD: It looks like a pig's foot.
MRS. OXFORD: That's what it is. I put it in the same sauce the French use for tripes.

Food and Sex

The Lady Vanishes

IRIS HENDERSON [Margaret Lockwood] (*to* GILBERT REDMAN [Michael Redgrave] *while waiting for her fiancé*): I could meet you for lunch or dinner, if you'd like it.

Suspicion

LINA MCLAIDLAW [Joan Fontaine] (*after being kissed for the first time*): Could I have some well done, please, Burton?

Vertigo

JUDY BARTON [Kim Novak] (*after making love with* JOHN

"SCOTTIE" FERGUSON [James Stewart]): I'm gonna have one of these beautiful steaks.

Spellbound
CONSTANCE PETERSEN [Ingrid Bergman] (*referring to the view*): Oh, isn't this beautiful?
JOHN BALLANTYNE [Gregory Peck] (*referring to* CONSTANCE *and then changing the conversation*): Perfect...Oh, lunch, lunch. What will you have? Ham or liverwurst?

Stage Fright
EVE GILL [Jane Wyman] (*referring to her sexual appetite for* JONATHAN COOPER [Richard Todd] *and pointing to her stomach*): When I'm with him, I get a feeling in here that, that's sort of—
COMMODORE GILL [Alastair Sim] (EVE'S *father*): We'll go into the symptoms later. Meanwhile, I'll take it you're rather keen on him or still hungry.
EVE: I'm in love with him.

EVE (*to* WILFRID SMITH [Michael Wilding]): But I'm sure you'd love to have some ice cream, and Chubby can show you where it is.
CHUBBY BANNISTER [Patricia Hitchcock] (*a friend of* EVE'S *who has hungry eyes for* WILFRID): But I'd adore to.

Notorious
ALICIA HUBERMAN [Ingrid Bergman] (*while she is kissing and seducing* DEVLIN [Cary Grant]): Let's stay here.
DEVLIN: We have to eat.
ALICIA: We'll eat here. I'll cook.
DEVLIN: I thought you didn't like to cook.
ALICIA: No, I don't like to cook, but I have a chicken in the icebox, and you're eating it.
DEVLIN: What about all the washing up afterward?
ALICIA: We'll eat it with our fingers.

ALEXANDER SEBASTIAN [Claude Rains] (*to* ALICIA, *whom he is trying to seduce*): What should we have for our first dinner together?

The Paradine Case

LORD HORFIELD [Charles Laughton]: You look very appetizing tonight, my dear.

GAY KEANE [Ann Todd]: A charming compliment from a gourmet such as yourself, Lord Horfield.

Rear Window

LISA FREEMONT [Grace Kelly]: Why don't I slip into something more comfortable?

L. B. JEFFRIES [James Stewart]: By all means.

LISA: I mean, like in the kitchen and make us some coffee.

To Catch a Thief

FRANCES STEVENS [Grace Kelly] (*referring to the fried chicken she brought on a picnic*): Do you want a leg or a breast?

JOHN ROBIE [Cary Grant]: You make the choice.

North by Northwest

ROGER O. THORNHILL [Cary Grant] (*dictating to his secretary a note to go with a box of candy to one of his girlfriends*): Oh, well, put "Something for your sweet tooth, baby, and your other sweet parts."

EVE KENDALL [Eva Marie Saint]: I never discuss love on an empty stomach.

ROGER: You've already eaten.

EVE: But you haven't.

EVE: Incidentally, I wouldn't order any dessert if I were you.

ROGER: I get the message.

EVE: That isn't exactly what I meant. This train seems to be making an unscheduled stop, and I saw two men getting out of

"If we ever get out of this alive, let's go back to New York on the train, alright?"

"Is that a proposition?"

"It's a proposal sweetie."

Cary Grant asks Eva Marie Saint to marry him while they're being chased by dangerous killers on top of Mount Rushmore in *North by Northwest*.

a police car as we pulled into the station. They weren't smiling.

EVE: You've got taste in clothes, taste in food...

ROGER: ...and taste in women. I like your flavor.

Psycho

SAM LOOMIS [John Gavin], who meets his girlfriend, MARION

CRANE [Janet Leigh] for sex on lunch hours: You never did eat your lunch, did you?

MARION: I better get back to the office. These extended lunch hours give my boss excess acid.

MRS. BATES: Go on! Go tell her she'll not be appeasing her ugly appetite with my food, or with my son!

Torn Curtain

MICHAEL ARMSTRONG [Paul Newman]: What are we going to do about lunch?

SARAH SHERMAN [Julie Andrews]: We haven't had breakfast yet.

MICHAEL (*referring to their lovemaking*): Well, we'll call this lunch and go upstairs for breakfast.

Food and Murder

Blackmail

MR WHITE [Charles Paton] (*to his daughter* ALICE [Anny Ondra], *who just murdered a man with a knife*): Alice, cut me a bit of bread, will you?

The 39 Steps

RICHARD HANNAY [Robert Donat]: Meanwhile, what are you going to do?

ANNABELLA SMITH [Lucie Mannheim], (before she is murdered): I'm going to eat my haddock.

MRS. JORDAN [Helen Haye]: I thought you were coming to lunch directly, dear. We've all been waiting. Will Mr. Hannay be joining us?

PROFESSOR JORDAN [Godfrey Tearle], who is planning on killing Hannay: I don't think so, dear.

Young and Innocent

In *Young and Innocent,* four brothers discuss over lunch the case of ROBERT TISDALL [Derrick de Marney], a man who's been accused of murder and who has managed to escape:

"I wonder what he bought with his last three shillings."

"Food, of course!"

"I know that. I meant, what kind of food."

"Sausages."

"The best thing would be chocolate. It has very good staying power."

"I suppose he didn't care going to a shop to get food."

"Then I'm afraid he'll be very hungry."

"And this, of course, may force him to come back."

"Unless he faints from hunger and dies in the fields."

Sabotage

A MAN (*who is planning the assassination of the* LORD MAYOR *and referring to a turtle in a fish tank*): It will take three like that to make soup at Lord Mayor's banquet next Saturday.

Rebecca

JACK FAVELL [George Sanders] (*while eating a leg of chicken and referring to* REBECCA's *mysterious death*): By the way, what do we do with old bones?

Notorious

ERIC MATHIS [Ivan Triesault] (*as he makes an exit to murder a man*): Thank you, Alex, for an excellent dinner, and please, tell your mother for me that the dessert was superb.

Shadow of a Doubt

EMMA NEWTON [Patricia Collinge] (*referring to her brother,* CHARLIE [Joseph Cotten], *a murderer*): I thought I'd make a maple cake. My brother, Charles loves maple cakes.

UNCLE CHARLIE (*after finding out another man has been accused of his crimes and has died*): Well, I think I'll go and get ready for dinner. I'm hungry. I could eat a good dinner today.

The Paradine Case
MRS. PARADINE [Valli] (*a woman who has murdered her husband, as she is being arrested*): Tell the cook I'm sorry about the dinner.

Rope
BRANDON [John Dall] (*referring to the candlesticks he placed on the chest in which he hid the body of his victim and from which he intends to serve food for a party*): I think they suggest a ceremonial altar which you can eat [at] with the foods for our sacrificial feast.

MRS. WILSON [Edith Evanson] (*referring to the chicken served on that very same chest*): You better get along with the carving.

RUPERT CADELL [James Stewart] (*to PHILIP [Farley Granger], who has murdered a friend with his friend, Brandon*): You're quite a good chicken strangler, as I recall.

RUPERT: Did you think you were God, Brandon? Is that what you thought when you choked the life out of him? Is that what you thought when you served food from his grave?

Strangers on a Train
BRUNO ANTHONY [Robert Walker] (*who portrays a killer*): Tell me, Judge, after you've sentenced a man to the chair, isn't it difficult to go out and have dinner after that?

I thought the lamb chops were a little overdone.

A YOUNG MAN (*to MIRIAM HAINES [Laura Elliot] before she is strangled*): I've never seen a girl eat so much in all my life.

The Trouble With Harry
CAPT. ALBERT WILES [Edmund Gwenn]: It takes a real cook to make good blueberry muffins, to keep the blueberries from sitting on the bottom.

MISS GRAVELEY [Mildred Natwick]: High-bush blueberries, that's the secret. I pick them up near where you shot that unfortunate man.

Suspicion
DR. BERTRAM SEDBUSK [Gavin Gordon] (*while eating chicken*): Ah! Arsenic! I remember in Gloucester, where we exhumed a body four year after, there will still enough poison in the fingernails and the hair.

Rear Window
STELLA [Thelma Ritter] (*to* L. B. JEFFRIES [James Stewart], *while he is eating his breakfast and drinking coffee and referring to the possible murder of a neighbor*): Just where do you suppose he cut her up? Of course, the bathtub. That's the only place where he could have washed away the blood. He better get that trunk out of there before it starts to leak.

Frenzy
INSPECTOR OXFORD [Alec McCowen] (*while eating his dinner and while his wife* [Vivien Merchant] *is breaking a breadstick*): The corpse was deep in rigor mortis. He had to break the fingers of the right hand to retrieve whatever held them.

To Catch a Thief
JOHN ROBIE [Cary Grant] (*referring to her cook*): Germaine has sensitive hands and an exceedingly light touch.
H. H. HUGHSON [John Williams]: Yes, I can tell.
JOHN : She strangled a German general all without a sound.
H. H. HUGHSON: Extraordinary woman...

North by Northwest
ROGER O. THORNHILL [Cary Grant] (*to two killers*): By the way, what are we having for dessert?

CLARA THORNHILL [Jessie Royce Landis] (*trying to get her son's attention while he is trying to escape from two killers*): Roger, Roger, will you be home for dinner?

Psycho

MARION CRANE [Janet Leigh] (*who is soon to be murdered*): I want to sleep more than anything else. Except maybe food.

NORMAN BATES [Anthony Perkins], a psychotic killer (*to MARION his next victim*): Would you have dinner with me? I was just about to myself. You know, nothing special. Just sandwiches and milk.

NORMAN: I really don't have much of an appetite.

MARION: But as long as you've fixed the supper, we might as well eat it.

NORMAN: Eating in an office is just—just too officious.

NORMAN: It's all for you. I'm not hungry. Go ahead. You—you eat like a bird.
MARION (*referring to NORMAN'S stuffed birds and hobby, taxidermy*): And you'd know, of course.
NORMAN: No, not really. Anyway, I hear the expression "eats like a bird,"—it—it's really a fals-fals-fals-falsity. Because birds really eat a tremendous lot.

MRS. CHAMBERS [Lurene Tuttle], *the SHERIFF'S wife,* (*to SAM LOOMIS [John Gavin] and LILA CRANE [Vera Miles] and referring to the report they have to file on LILA'S missing sister, MARION*): It's Sunday. Come on over to the house and do your reporting around dinnertime. It will make it nicer.

MRS. BATES (*to her son, NORMAN*): No, I will not hide in the fruit cellar. Ha, you think I'm fruity.

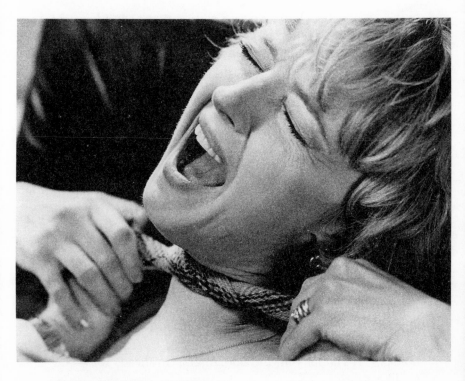

Barbara Leigh-Hunt in *Frenzy*.

"The murderer in *Frenzy* is a very cheerful fellow. Most people make murderers so sinister, they'd never get near the girl." —Hitchcock.

Frenzy

BOB RUSK [Barry Foster], a psychotic killer: Beulah, peel me a grape. That's what my mom used to say.

RUSK (who strangles his victims with ties and works at a fruit market): You know, in my trade, we have a saying; we put it on the fruit. "Don't squeeze the goods until they're yours." Now, that's me. I wouldn't ever do that.

Where the fruits come from, that's where I'd like to go if I wasn't tied down here.

I have my good points. I like flowers and fruit. People like me.

(*to one of his victims*): A very frugal lunch you've got there. Frugal and mean. Certainly not enough to support a lady with your opulent figure.
BRENDA BLANEY [Barbara Leigh-Hunt]: Rather too opulent I'm afraid these days, hence the frugality.

INSPECTOR OXFORD [Alec McCowen] (*referring to the killer*): We've got to find him before his appetite is whetted again.

JOHNNY PORTER [Clive Swift] (*referring to one of the victims*): They found her in a potato bag.

MRS. OXFORD [Vivien Merchant] (*referring to* RICHARD BLANEY [Jon Finch], *a man who has finally been cleared of murders he didn't commit*): I think the best you could do is ask him around for a very good dinner. Let's see, it would obviously have to be something substantial. I think a *caneton aux cerises*.
INSPECTOR OXFORD: What's that?
MRS. OXFORD: Duckling with heavy, sweet cherry sauce.
INSPECTOR OXFORD: Well, after that jail food he's been having, I expect he'll eat anything.

Young and Innocent
ERICA BURGOYNE [Nova Pilbeam] (*to her father* [Percy Marmont] *a detective who has wrongly accused* ROBERT TISDALL [Derrick de Marney] *of murder*): Don't you think we ought to invite Mr. Tisdall to dinner?

Family Plot

FRAN [Karen Black] (*to* ARTHUR ADAMSON [William Devane], *her boyfriend who wants her to help him commit a murder*): It's my stomach, Arthur. Murder doesn't agree with it.

Also on the Menu...

The Lodger (*title card*)

THE LODGER [Ivor Novello]: Nothing more, please, just some bread and butter and a glass of milk.

Number Seventeen

THE DETECTIVE [John Stuart]: Well, you better come along with me.

THE GIRL [Anne Grey] (*thinking she is being arrested*): Where?

THE DETECTIVE: To have some breakfast!

The Man Who Knew Too Much (1934)

JILL LAWRENCE [Edna Best] (*on the phone to her daughter* [Nova Pilbeam] *who's been kidnapped*): Are you alright? Plenty of food?

Sabotage

VERLOC [Oscar Homolka]: Always that woman, Mrs. Jones, manages to make cabbage green.

MRS. VERLOC [Sylvia Sidney]: I'm always telling her you like things green. I'll make you a salad.

TED SPENSER [John Loder]: Good evening, Mrs. Verloc. For-give me for butting into your personal affairs, but this bright specimen did not know whether he wanted long, round, square, or oblong lettuce. I brought a selection.

TED'S code words for his colleague to follow VERLOC a man suspected of sabotage: Peach, pineapple! Pineapple, Peach!

RENEE [Joyce Barbour] (*a cashier at a movie theatre and who is late because of a blackout*): So sorry, Mrs. Verloc, but I had a hell of a time to eat my eggs on toast in the dark.

STEVIE [Desmond Tester] (*referring to* TED SPENSER): He is too dignified to eat eggs.

TED: Poached eggs, here at Simpson's? Well, it's enough to make the roast beef turn until it's gravy!

The Lady Vanishes

IRIS HENDERSON [Margaret Lockwood]: What is it, Boris?
BORIS [Emile Boreo], *the hotel manager*: The *have lunch!*
JULIE [Sally Stewart] (IRIS'*s friend*): Have a lunch?
IRIS: Avalanche, Boris. Avalanche.

BORIS: There is no 'eating on the train.
CALDICOTT [Naunton Wayne]: No eating on the train?
BORIS: Yes, I mean, no heating. Brr...

BLANCHE [Googie Withers] (IRIS'*s friend*): And speaking of wind, we haven't eaten since dawn.
IRIS: Serve us supper, Boris, in our room.
JULIE: I could eat a horse.
IRIS: Don't put any idea in his head. Er...some chicken, Boris, and a magnum of champagne.

CHARTERS [Basil Radford]: Well, what do you say to a grilled steak?
CALDICOTT: A very good idea. Well done for me, please.
CHARTERS: On the red side for me.

MISS FROY [Dame May Whitty]: He is trying to explain to you that owing to the large numbers of visitors, there is no food left.
CHARTERS: No food? What sort of place is this? Do they

expect us to share a blasted dog box with a servant girl on an empty stomach?

GILBERT REDMAN [Michael Redgrave]: What was she dressed in? Scotch tweeds, wasn't it?
IRIS: Oatmeal tweeds.
GILBERT: I knew it had something to do with porridge.

GILBERT: Do you think you could eat anything?
IRIS: I could try.
GILBERT: That's the spirit. You'll feel a different girl tomorrow.

Rebecca
SHE [Joan Fontaine]: I'm sorry, I'm not very hungry.
MAXIM DE WINTER [Laurence Olivier]: Come on. Eat it up like a good girl.

FRITZ THE BUTLER [Edward Fielding]: Isn't there anything I could get for you, madame?
SHE: Oh, no, thank you, Fritz. I'm really not very hungry.

MRS. VAN HOPPER [Florence Bates] (*after taking cold medicine*): Wretched stuff! Give me a chocolate, quick!

MRS. DANVERS [Dame Judith Anderson]: I'd like to know if you approve of the menu.
SHE: Oh, well...Well, I'm sure it's very suitable. Very nice indeed.
MRS. DANVERS: You noticed, madame, that I left a blank space for the sauce. Mrs. de Winter was most particular about sauces.

Spellbound
JOHN BALLANTYNE [Gregory Peck] (*to* CONSTANCE PETERSEN

[Ingrid Bergman]): Kleptomaniacs for lunch. They'll steal the food right out of your mouth.

CONSTANCE [to John]: I'm glad you didn't dream about me as an egg beater, as one of my patients did.

Shadow of a Doubt
EMMA NEWTON [Patricia Collinge]: You don't start a cake by breaking an egg. You put the butter and sugar in first. You see, after all, survey or no survey, I'm not going to start by breaking an egg.

EMMA (*referring to her neighbor* HERB HAWKINS [Hume Cronyn]: Joe, it's Herbert...He always comes when we're eating.

JOE NEWTON [Henry Travers]: Had your dinner?
HERB: I had mine an hour ago. You folks are getting pretty stylish, having dinner later every evening.

EMMA (*serving one of her guests*): Mrs. Potter...Oh, don't take that one, I don't know why I make tomatoes. They always soak through the bread when they've been standing. Try one of these. It's just whole-wheat bread and cream cheese. It's the paprika that makes it pink.

Lifeboat
KOVAC [John Hodiak] (*to* CONSTANCE PORTER [Tallulah Bankhead]): When you write your book, it will make a swell chapter. How it feels to be hungry. First person singular. That's a good thing to write about, hunger and thirst.

The Paradine Case
LORD HORFIELD [Charles Laughton]: It is surprising how closely the convulsions of a walnut resemble those of the human brain.

Rope

MRS. WILSON [Edith Evanson] (*to* PHILIP [Farley Granger]): Well, now, mind you. Don't be so busy at that piano that you don't eat anything. Getting too thin. And don't let them gobble up all that pâté before you have any.

MRS. WILSON (*to* JANET WALKER [Joan Chandler]): If I were you, I'd go easy on the pâté. Calories.

Under Capricorn

CHARLES ADARE [Michael Wilding] (*to* LADY HENRIETTA FLUSKY [Ingrid Bergman] *while trying to convince her to be the lady of her house*): Let me see. What's the first battle? I know, the kitchen.

LADY HENRIETTA FLUSKY (*giving orders to her cooks*): You three make breakfast. I want coffee, toast, eggs, and bacon. Three separate breakfasts. Each of you will make one breakfast, and the one who does best will be the cook.

Dial M for Murder

TONY WENDICE [Ray Milland]: I'm so glad we don't have to go to Maureen's. She is such a filthy cook.

Rear Window

LISA FREEMONT [Grace Kelly]: I guess I better start setting up the dinner.

LISA (*to* L. B. JEFFRIES [James Stewart] *after they have had a lovers' quarrel*): At least you can't say the dinner isn't right.

JEFFRIES (*trying to explain to* LISA *why she could never come with him on his photo-shoot assignments around the globe*): Did you ever eat fish heads and rice?
LISA: Of course not.

JEFFRIES: You might have to if you went with me.

And later, using the same subject to discourage LISA
JEFFRIES: And sometimes the food you eat is made from things that you couldn't even look at when they were alive.

The Trouble With Harry
SAM MARLOWE [John Forsythe], who has just sold his paintings to a millionaire [Parker Fennelly] and decides to give his future girlfriend, JENNIFER ROGERS [Shirley MacLaine], a present of her choice: What do you like most in the whole world?

JENNIFER: I don't know. Strawberries, I guess.
SAM: Strawberries. Write that down. Two boxes of fresh strawberries, first of each month, in season and out of season from now on.

The Man Who Knew Too Much (1956)
HANK MCKENNA [Christopher Olsen] (*referring to the snails in his parents' backyard*): We tried everything to get rid of them. We never thought of a Frenchman.

BEN MCKENNA [James Stewart] (*referring to bread at a restaurant in Morocco*): Does it chew better than it tastes?
JO [Doris Day], Ben's wife, has other concerns about the bread: Is it fattening?

BEN (*after being unable to eat his meal with his hands*): I'll practice on an olive.

BEN: Where is my boy, Drayton?
MR. DRAYTON [Bernard Miles], who has kidnapped BEN'S son: He's upstairs. As a matter of fact, you've come just in time to help my wife with his food. It seems Hank doesn't care very much for our English cooking.

North by Northwest

ROGER O. THORNHILL [Cary Grant] (*to his secretary*): You know that's your trouble, Maggie, you don't eat properly.

ROGER: Do you recommend anything?
EVE KENDALL [Eva Marie Saint]: The brook trout. A little trouty but quite good.

The Birds

MITCH BRENNER [Rod Taylor]: What time is dinner, Mother?
LYDIA [Jessica Tandy]: Seven o'clock. Same as usual.

MITCH (to MELANIE DANIELS [Tippi Hedren]): Then stay and have something to eat before you start back. I'd feel a lot better.

MRS. BUNDY [Ethel Griffies], a customer at a dinner: Birds are not aggressive creatures, miss. They bring beauty into the world. It is mankind—(interrupted by the waitress placing an order): Sam, two southern fried chickens, baked potato on all of them!

Marnie

MARNIE EDGAR [Tippi Hedren] (*to her mother,* BERNICE [Louise Latham], *and referring to the pecan pie she is cooking for a neighbor she loathes*): After all, it is Jessie's pie, isn't it?

Topaz

A SPY, Hernandez [Carlos Rivas] (*referring to the camera hidden between two slices of bread*): We must make sure that Pablo does not eat the camera!

Family Plot

FRAN [Karen Black] (*referring to the man she and* ARTHUR ADAMSON [William Devane] *kidnapped and released*): Mr. Constantine has left us some wine.

ARTHUR: I don't think he likes the imported stuff.
FRAN: It's probably my veal parmigiana. I'm afraid I over-cooked it.

A DETECTIVE (*talking to the victim of a kidnapping*): Who did the cooking?
CONSTANTINE [Nicholas Colasanto]: She did.
DETECTIVE: Why?
CONSTANTINE: Because a man would not bother to put the parsley on the filet of sole, that's why!

ARTHUR (*referring to* BISHOP WOODS [William Prince], another one of his kidnap victims): Anything wrong with our houseguest?
FRAN: He's fine. I gave him a very nice lunch and a fresh bottle of wine.

ARTHUR: Bishop Woods, it's time to go. Have your vestments on?
WOODS: Yes, but I haven't finished the chicken.

BLANCHE TAYLOR [Barbara Harris] (*to her boyfriend,* GEORGE LUMLEY [Bruce Dern]): Ifs, darling, you're always giving me ifs. I can't eat ifs, and neither can you.

BLANCHE: What do you think?
GEORGE: It smells fishy to me.
BLANCHE: Even fish smells good when you're starving.

Hitch: The Man Who Knew So Much

When Hitchcock began his career during the silent era, filmmaking was still at an experimental stage. The camera was the only tool a director had to convey a story; title cards had to be kept to a minimum. While directors were still adjusting to the possibilities this new medium offered, movies started to talk. It was 1929, and Hitchcock had just completed directing *Blackmail,* his tenth picture in England* and his second thriller. In terms of history, Hitchcock was at an important crossroad. John Maxwell, the producer of *Blackmail,* set up a temporary sound stage with RCA material imported from America. It was then very costly and technically difficult to add post-dubbing. So Hitchcock had to reshoot part of the film with live music and offstage sound effects. But the leading actress in the film, Anny Ondra, was Czech and German and had an accent you could cut with a knife. Hitchcock had to hire another actress named Joan Barry to speak Anny Ondra's Cockney lines off-camera while Ondra mouthed them in front of the camera. Nothing stopped

---

*One, *Number 13*, was unfinished.

Hitchcock, and as he continued to pursue his career, he literally invented a filmmaking encyclopedia.

Hitchcock's camera shots were complex. So was he. His quotes about himself, his education, even his childhood, are directly linked to his views on filmmaking and to his understanding of his audience and are transcended through the love-hate relationship he had with actors. The following quotes by Hitchcock are excerpted from articles only and sum up how Hitchcock defined himself, filmmaking, the public, and actors.

Hitchcock on Himself

"It's been my observation that a man does not live by murder alone. He needs affection, approval, encouragement, and occasionally, a hearty meal."

Regarding his famous outline: "I drew it myself. I began to draw it years ago, when I was a movie art director. With one exception, there's been little change in it since then. At one time, I had more hair. All three of them were wavy."

"I was third or fourth at school. It's better than coming first. When you are first, people expect too much, and then the strain is very great."

"I was Jesuit educated. The only thing I learned was fear."

"I was born a Catholic. I went to Catholic school, and now I have a conscience with lots of trial over beliefs."

"The only thing about my Jesuit education is that I was scared to hell the whole time I was there. Maybe that's how I learned fear."

"Don't let any priests on the lot. They're after me; they all hate me."

"I have no friends who are actors or directors, and my wife and I spend as much time as possible away from Hollywood in our own country home in northern California."

"My wife cooks every night, and I help her wash up."

"Despite all my bluster and bravado, I'm really quite sensitive and cowardly. I'm terrified of policemen."

"When I go on a diet, which I often do, Alma faithfully loses weight with me, although she's not quite five feet and weighs less than a hundred pounds."

"Contrary to what one would think from my measurements, I'm not a heavy eater. I'm simply one of those unfortunates who can accidentally swallow a cashew nut and put on thirty pounds right away."

"Let us say that I indulged in everything generously. You know, you don't put on weight thinking about food."

"A New York doctor once told me that I'm an adrenal type. That apparently means that I'm all body and only vestigial legs. But since I'm neither a mile runner nor a dancer and my present interest in my body is almost altogether from the waist up, that didn't bother me much."

"I daresay than any man who names his dog Phillip of Magnesia, as I did, is hard to live with."

"I just think Jeffrey and Stanley are rather nice names for dogs. If I had a son, I'm sure I'd call him Rover."

"I do have a sense of humor. I've been scaring everybody for forty-six years. You have to have a sense of humor to survive that."

"I don't believe in the theory of trying to top yourself."

"I'm one of the most meticulous, orderly people you'll ever meet. There is even an orderly logic in my dreams."

"I don't believe in practical jokes that hurt anyone, only bewilder them."

"If the joke is a proper one, the victim should remain on friendly terms with the perpetrator."

Referring to Los Angeles: "The place is all right, but it isn't easy to understand the people."

Question: "Why do you like working in Hollywood?"
Hitchcock: "Because I can get home at six o'clock for dinner."

"What I want is a home, not a movie set with a heating plant added. All I need is a snug little house, with a good kitchen, and the devil with a swimming pool."

"I owe my longetivity to a placid metabolism."

"I sometimes think, though, I would have liked to have been a criminal lawyer. Think of the opportunity I would have had to be a great man in court."

"Politics is none of my business."

Question: "Do you regard yourself as a liberal?"
Answer: "I think I am in every sense of the term. I was

recently asked whether I was a Democrat. I answered that I was a Democrat, but in respect to my money, I am a Republican. I am not a hypocrite."

Hitch's motto: "We are all criminals, we who watch. We are all Peeping Toms. And we follow the Eleventh Commandment: 'Thou shalt not be found out.'"

"I've spent all my life trying to avoid clichés."

"I haven't given a thought to when I retire."

"I have nothing to retire for. Age doesn't matter. I think it's a state of mind that you live with from the waist up."

"When people say I'm seventy, I say that's a confounded lie. I'm twice thirty-five, that's all. Twice thirty-five."

Hitchcock on Filmmaking

"My first script was about a shell-shocked British officer and a French dancer who turned up with child. I was twenty-three and an uncommonly unattractive young man, and I had never been out with a girl in my life. With my background, I barely knew how the dancer got to be with child."

"I was deeply interested in film from about twelve or fourteen on."

The traditional Hitchcock film: "It encompasses true horror and comedy at the same time."

Referring to the McGuffin, the mysterious element of the plot: "There is a bloke on a train. He sees a package and asks what it is. Man says it's a McGuffin. Other man asks, what is a McGuffin? Other cove says a McGuffin is an apparatus for trapping lions in the Adirondacks. But there are no lions in the Adirondacks, the other bloke says. Then this thing is no McGuffin, second lad says."

"The McGuffin is the thing that the spies are after but the audience don't care."

"Self-plagiarism is style."

"Drama is life with the dull bits left out."

"Melodrama is not an exaggeration of real life but a reasonable facsimile of it."

"All things considered, I think I'm doing well if I get the sixty percent of my original conception on the screen."

"You start with a good idea and you work it over into a picture. If the finished product is seventy-five percent as good as you originally thought it would be, you've done as well as possible."

"I would say the chase is almost indigenous to movie technique as a whole."

"In many ways the chase makes up about sixty percent of the construction of all movie plots."

"In the ideal chase structure, the tempo and complexity of the chase will be an accurate reflection of the intensity of the relations between the characters."

"D. W. Griffith was the first to exploit the possibilities of the chase."

"I have derived more from novelists like John Buchan, J. B.

Priestley, John Galsworthy, and Mrs. Belloc-Lowndes than from the movies. I like them because they use multiple chases and a lot of psychology. My chases are the result of using all the resources of modern film techniques to combine what I got from these novelists with what I got from Griffith."

"I shoot a precut picture."

"I always thought films were financed from the receipts of the previous film."

"I don't decry dialogue, but I feel that technique is not necessary cinematic."

"The cinema is a succession of images put together like a sentence."

"The length of a film should be directly related to the endurance of the human bladder."

"Making a film is just realizing what you have on paper by coming onstage and physically putting it in the can."

"Cinema is telling stories in pictures and cutting."

"For me, cinema is essentially emotion."

"All moviemaking is pure montage."

"A camera has a language all its own."

"A motion picture makes a statement by visual means."

"A filmmaker isn't supposed to say things. He's supposed to show them."

"In a good movie, the sound could go off and the audience would still have a perfectly clear idea of what was going on."

"Editing is crucial. Imagine James Stewart looking at a mother nursing a child. You see the child, then cut back to him. Now Mr. Stewart is a benign old gentleman. Take away the middle piece of film and substitute a girl in a bikini. Now he's dirty old man."

"Technique should enrich the action."

"The true art of film is not photographs of people talking. It is little pieces of film glued together which are run through a projection machine onto a screen, and the succession of images creates an illusion for the audience—that's what true film is all about, but it's rarely practiced."

"Directing a film to me is not just lining up shots and going home. It's involving myself in every aspect of the film right from the time I search for locations, just as an author would do for a book, until the fine shadings of dubbing, music, and effects."

"Learn the art and craft of filmmaking on paper first as a composer learns the technique of writing music. Master every aspect of it in theory and then put what you've learned into practice."

"The only thing that will kill off a movie mogul is extreme old age."

"In this community, to have what is known as an unhappy ending is to commit the unforgivable Hollywood sin called 'being downbeat.'"

"I suppose I must be honest and say it is very pleasant when the film is good, but it is very unpleasant when the picture is a failure. Frankly, it's miserable!"

"I just don't think the new people get as much training as we did in the old days."

"A lot of people embrace the auteur theory. But it's difficult to know what someone means by it. I suppose they mean that the responsibility for the film rests solely on the shoulders of the director. But very often the director is no better than his script."

"I don't need to look through the camera; that's only for an amateur. It's easy enough to tell a cameraman what you want in that white rectangle."

"The simple and more homely the peril, the more real the peril."

"I think films should be tied off, and not necessarily happily."

"I've always said that in structuring a film, you may leave certain holes in the early part, so long as you plug that hole before the film ends. You don't have to be what I call 'logical,' which is very dull, and plug a hole right at the moment it is expected."

"The first thing I throw out is logic."

"Truffaut tried to follow my work when he made *The Bride Wore Black*, you see, and he misunderstood my dictum that logic is dull when you use too much footage trying to explain a point."

"The fact is I practice absurdity quite religiously."

"It's been said of my stories that they are so tightly knit that everything depends on everything else and that if I ever made a change before the camera, I might as well unravel the whole sweater."

"The wide screen was an additional comfort, like plusher carpet or better velvet on the seats."

"When you have a nightmare, you use the word 'vivid.' Well, that's what the film has to be so that you're glad when you wake up on your way to the guillotine."

"There is no terror in a bang, only in the anticipation of it."

"It is the way fear is treated that makes for good box office, not the actual fear itself—and it is box office that counts money."

"Most films should be seen through more than once."

"I can't tell a story if I don't start at the beginning and finish at the end."

"I'm not much of a moviegoer."

"No one in a costume picture ever goes to the toilet."

Referring to his film *The Lodger*: "One day I was a flop, all washed up at the age of twenty-six; the next day, I was a boy genius. So you can see I've had some personal experience in the field of suspense."

"*Shadow of a Doubt* is my favorite because there is really a combination of character, suspense, and atmosphere."

"I did a dialogue film, *Dial M for Murder*, which was taken from a successful play. I could have phoned that one in."

"*Rear Window* is pure motion picture, even though the man never moves from one position."

"*The Trouble With Harry* was one of my favorite films and still is, and yet it lost money because I was doing something that pleased me."

"There are no symbols in *North by Northwest*. Oh, yes! The last shot. The train entering the tunnel after the love scene between Grant and Eva Marie Saint. It's a phallic symbol. But don't tell anyone!"

"To me *Psycho* was a big comedy. Had to be."

"Thirty-three percent of the effect of *Psycho* was due to the music."

"Even my failures make money and become classics a year after I make them."

"I haven't seen *A Clockwork Orange*, but I know I wouldn't go for that kind of violence."

But Hitchcock later changed his mind: "I thought was an interesting picture." [A CLOCKWORK ORANGE]

"Truffaut said the one thing he learned from me was the use of the camera as a subjective thing."

Referring to David O. Selznick, who produced *Rebecca*, *Spellbound*, *Notorious*, and *The Paradine Case:* "Well, he was the Big Producer."

"The most flattering thing Mr. Selznick ever said about me— and it shows you the amount of control—he said I was 'the only director he'd trust with a film.'"

"When I came to America twenty-five years ago to direct *Rebecca*, David Selznick sent me a memo. I've just finished reading it. I think I may turn it into a motion picture. I plan to call it *The Longest Story Ever Told*."

Note: Producer David O. Selznick was famous for writing lengthy memos to everyone involved in the production of his films.

"I want to be remembered as a man who entertained millions through the technique of film."

Hitchcock and the Audience

"I don't put my personal feelings into pictures. I don't indulge myself. I don't make pictures to please me. I make them to please the audience."

"Always make the audience suffer as much as possible."

"Make the audience suffer in their soft, comfortable seats as they see the characters of the drama grope for solutions which the audiences already know."

"Another thing I'm afraid of is going to see any of my pictures with an audience present. I only tried that once, with *To Catch a Thief*, and I was a wreck. I'm scared of seeing the mistakes I might have made."

"The critics aren't often perceptive about film. Some of them tend to judge a picture on its content. But content isn't everything. It's treatment, style, and the handling of it that creates an emotion in an audience."

"It is my hope that audiences will be willing to accept a little freshness of treatment now and then. They can't be that conditioned!"

"People will go to the movies as long as you give them stories."

"In a serious chase, when you have comic relief, it's important that the hero as well as the audience be relieved."

"In respect to audiences, I have found that there are certain things we can always count on the audience to feel, so long as they can count on us, too."

"If you show too much, you don't scare the audience. You just nauseate them."

"Violence for the sake of violence I don't think has any effect. I don't even think the audience is moved by it."

"Give an audience too much sex—or in bad taste—and they become embarrassed or laugh at the wrong place. The trick is to time the reaction; give them something you want them to laugh at."

"When employing suspense, you have to give the audience a chance to laugh. If you don't, the human body cannot stand the strain, and the whole affair will become ludicrous."

"The suspense element can be just as upsetting as the most horrific film. You arrive at suspense by letting the audience in."

"The technique of motion pictures is unique, and whatever people may say, it is still a wonderful medium for bringing the people and backgrounds of the farthest points of the world into neighborhood motion picture theaters."

"My interest in doing motion pictures and TV is to satisfy myself artistically and, yes, to give satisfaction to audiences all over the world who want a return for the admission price they plunk down or the time they invest with you."

"I found that viewers cared more for a little anxiety in their film fare than they did for some of the other dramatic qualities. So I continued, and I don't mind saying that I like it pretty much myself."

"Everything must be very clear to the audience. Too often filmmakers present such complicated scenes and plots, they lose their audience."

"I can hear them scream when I'm making the picture."

"When you can hear the audience screaming, it's no different from a man who designs roller coasters."

"I've been called a ghoul, but I know when an audience is going to scream. I enjoy it, and I have to smile to myself in anticipation of what I'm doing to them."

"I don't care about the subject matter; I don't care about the acting; but I do care about the pieces of film—all the technical ingredients that make the audience scream."

"I always take the audience into account."

"Realism is very important, because audiences catch mistakes, but it must occasionally be sacrificed for the pictorial effect."

"People like to apply the solution of the plot to their own problems."

"People who arrive when a picture is on should not be admitted until next time round."

"People don't want to sit around home to see the kind of program now being televised. After the novelty has worn off, they'll go back to the movies, where they can get the kind of entertainment that never will be televised until the film industry does it."

On the future of the movies: "No radical change until there is a change in audiences. This can come only from the class-room; it's a job for educators, not moviemakers. When audiences have advanced further, Hollywood will be ready to present them with advanced entertainment."

"If I seem doomed to make only one type of picture, the movie audience is responsible. People go to one of my films expect-ing a thriller, and they aren't satisfied until the thrill turns up."

"If an audience sees one of my productions with no spine tingling, they're disappointed."

"My name must be connected with some indication of horror. If I made a musical, I am sure the audience would wonder which of the chorus girls I am going to shoot."

"I'm so typed by the public that if I were to try my hand at another type of picture, let us say, a musical, I feel sure people would expect the soprano, when she reached her top C, to turn into a scream.

"It has been said of me that if I made *Cinderella,* the audience would start looking for a body in the pumpkin coach."

"A good film is that which absorbs the audience's attention

and enables them to come out of the theater and say, 'The dinner, the babysitter, the price of admission—that was all worth it.'"

Hitchcock on Acting

Regarding his cameo appearances: "It all started with a shortage of extras in my first thriller [*The Lodger*]. I was in for a few seconds as an editor with my back to the camera. It wasn't really much, but I played it to the hilt. Since then, I have been trying to get into every one of my pictures. It isn't that I like the business, but it has an impelling fascination that I can't resist. When I do it, the cast, the grips, and the cameramen and everyone else gather to make it as difficult as possible for me. But I can't stop now."

"I've always said to the cameraman to make it as short as you can so I don't suffer the indignity of being an actor too long."

"I like to get this gimmick over with early in a film. I don't want people to sit there just looking for me."

"Actors are cattle."

"I didn't say actors are cattle. What I said was, actors should be treated like cattle."

"I used to envy Walt Disney when he made only cartoons. If he didn't like an actor, he could just tear him up."

"I find it easier to work with actors who don't give me any trouble."

"If an actor gives me trouble, I just tell him, 'You do what you like. There's always the cutting-room floor.' And when you're on the cutting-room floor, you get trodden upon."

"When an actor comes to me and wants to discuss his character, I say, 'It's in the script.' If he says, 'But what's my motivation?,' I say, 'Your salary.'"

"I suppose I'm a coward in a way. I never have a row with an actor. I don't bawl him out or do anything of that kind."

"The best casting director is the novelist, because he can describe in words every facet and every thought of his characters."

"Actors really are like children, you know. That's why you get such a tremendous number of divorces in Hollywood. The participants in a love scene take their roles so seriously that they continue the scene after six o'clock in the dressing room. Such children!"

"They're nice children. They need to be petted and guided and should be patted on the head. Occasionally, they need a good spanking, too."

"I don't direct them. I talk to them and explain to them what the scene is, what its purpose is, why they are doing certain things—because they relate to the story, not to the scene."

"The most important thing is to get the actor to look in the right direction. If you've got a Method actor, you're in trouble, because he'll only look where he feels."

"The unknown cast is ideal because the audience comes in without preconceptions."

"The virtue of having unknowns is that then there's a greater realism about the whole piece."

"The story you are telling is always improved when the hero or the heroine who is in dire straits is well known: the onlookers experience a greater emotion from seeing a 'relative' in trouble than they would from seeing a stranger. Big-name stars have become familiar to moviegoers and therefore are like relatives to them."

"As for the cast, I'm not particular about having big stars as long as I know that my actors have sufficient experience."

"The star system is not an insurance. The star is good if the picture is good."

Referring to Cary Grant, who starred in *Suspicion, Notorious, To Catch a Thief,* and *North by Northwest:* "When you want an audience to have a very specific rooting interest in your hero, you'll get more if the figure is familiar, like Cary Grant."

"Once you decide to go after Cary Grant, the question of suitability takes second place to the question of availability."

"Cary is marvelous, you see. One doesn't direct Cary Grant; one simply puts him in front of the camera."

Referring to Grace Kelly, who starred in *Dial M for Murder, Rear Window,* and *To Catch a Thief:* "They all said at first she was too cold, sexless. But to me she always was, and still is, a snow-covered volcano."

"Remember Grace Kelly in *High Noon?* She was rather mousy. But in *Dial M for Murder,* she blossomed out for me splendidly, because the touch of elegance had always been there."

Referring to Laurence Olivier, who starred in *Rebecca:* "I think when Sir Laurence went into the theater, motion pictures lost one of the great romantic stars of our time."

Referring to Charles Laughton, who starred in Hitchcock's

Jamaica Inn and *The Paradine Case:* "You can't direct a Laughton picture. The best you can hope for is to referee."

"Charles Laughton was not a Method actor but used to behave like one. In *Jamaica Inn* we couldn't film him below the waist for ten days because he hadn't got the character's walk."

Referring to Ingrid Bergman, who starred in *Spellbound*, *Notorious*, and *Under Capricorn:* "You take a woman like Ingrid Bergman. She was what we called an apple-cheeked peasant girl when she first came here."

Hitchcock to Bergman: "Ingrid, it's only a movie!"

Referring to James Stewart (*Rope, Rear Window, The Man Who Knew Too Much, Vertigo*), who had trouble adjusting to the long takes on *Rope:* "He couldn't sleep nights because of the picture. It was the bewildering technique that made him worry."

Referring to Tippi Hedren, who starred in *The Birds* and *Marnie:* "I got an unexpected bonus. She memorized and read lines extraordinarily well. And she had nothing to unlearn as an actress because she had never acted before."

"I adored Carole Lombard—so much, in fact, that she was able to persuade me to do something outside my type, a bedroom farce called *Mr. and Mrs. Smith.*"

Referring to Tallulah Bankhead, who starred in *Lifeboat:* "Tallulah was a real pro, but I must say that she was tremendously extroverted. There were complaints that she was climbing in and out of the bright lights with nothing under her skirt."

Referring to Montgomery Clift, who starred in *I Confess:*

"Working with Montgomery Clift was difficult because, you know, he was a Method actor and neurotic as well."

Referring to Eva Marie Saint, who starred in *North by Northwest:* "I took a lot of trouble with Eva Marie Saint, grooming and making her appearance soignée. Next thing, she's in a picture called *Exodus* and looking like hell."

Referring to Julie Andrews, who starred in *Torn Curtain:* "The great mistake there was in casting Julie Andrews, but I let them talk me into it because she was so hot at the time. Then everybody sat around waiting for her to sing."

"Marilyn Monroe, for instance, if I ever have her for a picture, I'll start her out as a nun." [Marilyn Monroe never made a film with Hitchcock.]

In 1962, François Truffaut was promoting his film *Jules and Jim* in America. During a press conference, a journalist asked Truffaut why he took Hitchcock so seriously. "He's rich and successful, but his movies have no substance," the journalist claimed. He then basically told the French director that the reason why he loved *Rear Window* was because, as a foreigner, he knew nothing about Greenwich Village, where the story took place. To this comment, Truffaut replied: "*Rear Window* is not about Greenwich Village. It is a film about cinema, and I do know cinema." Truffaut wanted to write a book on Hitchcock because he felt the director had been mistreated and victimized by the critics. Hitchcock was, and still is, the most talked about director. Because he was notoriously difficult with his cast, actors who starred in his films would be asked to confirm or refute the legends surrounding Hitchcock. The quotes by actors who worked with Hitchcock are divided into three groups. An actress has been chosen to represent each period: The British years are introduced by Sylvia Sidney (*Sabotage*); the early American years, by Joan Fontaine (who received an Oscar nomination for *Rebecca* and received the gold statuette for best actress for her performance in *Suspicion*); and the later American year, by Janet Leigh (*Psycho*). These actresses were interviewed exclusively for this book. The last section in this chapter presents, in alphabetical order quotes on Hitchcock by some of his collaborators, his wife and his daughter, and by others who never knew him or worked with him but had something to say about Hitchcock.

Actors: The British Years

Sylvia Sidney (*Sabotage*):
"He had a fine reputation. He was a sort of cultural figure. He was a very talented young director who showed a lot of promises. He was starting to get a lot of recognition even in the States. When I was contacted to do *Sabotage*, I was very flattered and excited. I was one of the first American stars to go abroad to do a film."

"Hitchcock didn't shoot long scenes. He shot each sequence in little bits according to the way he intended to edit the picture."

"He thought that actors got in his way when they wanted him to make changes in a scene, because he was so well prepared and had already all his camera angles set up in his mind. During the shooting, he was very involved at getting things the way he needed them to be."

"Everybody seems surprised that I was not victimized by him in any way. . . . You know, like he did with Madeleine Carroll, for example. The only way I could figure out why he was so respectful toward me was the fact that I was making so much more money than him! He was notorious for having great consideration for the coin."

"I had a small altercation with Hitchcock over something in the film. I immediately went to Ivor Montagu, the producer of the film, and he just said to me, 'Trust him,' and explained that Hitchcock's results were always fine so I shouldn't worry about anything."

"I remember watching the film and being shocked by the fact that I played a woman who murders her husband and who walks out into the night with a future lover who happens to be a detective! I have no idea how Hitchcock got away with this, because I found the plot immoral. I think she should have paid for the crime."

Sir John Gielgud (*The Secret Agent*): "Alfred Hitchcock has often made me feel like jelly, and I have been nearly sick with nervousness."

Derrick de Marney (*Young and Innocent*): "Hitccock's eyes on the set are generally closed. He's been known to take catnaps even during shooting."

Michael Redgrave (*The Lady Vanishes*): "Everyone knew that his reputation here in England was more for preparation and technique than for working with his cast."

Margaret Lockwood (*The Lady Vanishes*): "He never really mixed with the actors. He knew exactly what he wanted, where the camera had to be set up. So you did what he wanted; that was it! I could speak for hours with Carol Reed, but Hitch..."

The Early American Years

Joan Fontaine (*Rebecca, Suspicion*):
"Hitchcock was absolutely like a father to me. He was kind, dear, and a family man. He loved to get his actresses drunk at his dinner parties and see them misbehave. That amused me. I'm sure that his alleged lustful attitude toward his actresses was set along those lines, too."

"His remark 'actors are cattle' was capricious humor."

"He was just a sweet 'roly-poly' man. He made it easy for me. He took all my nerves away. I felt a kindness and an understanding."

"He guided me all the way. I didn't have any problems, nor any concerns—just implicit trust."

"There was a scene in *Rebecca* when Judith Anderson tried to force me out a window. I was 'cried out.' We had done many takes the day before, and I just had no more tears left. So I asked Hitchcock to slap me in the face! It was wonderful of him to understand and ask the set for complete silence before the take as he did so. I think his loving understanding brought the flood of tears rather than the pain."

"I knew him well, and he never lost interest in his work. He was a perfectionist."

"Hitchcock had a large sketchbook beside him in his director chair. He would take it out and show the cameraman and myself what he wanted."

"He called me 'kid.'"

"He had great respect for women. He was very close to his wife and adored her and his daughter, Patricia. He was easygoing, almost placid. The only time he ever raised his voice was to say something humorous."

Laurence Olivier (*Rebecca*): "I admired and liked Hitchcock tremendously, and we had a jolly time; all English pros together. He didn't treat us like cattle, although he boasted that that was what he thought about all actors and although my leading lady docilely obeyed him like a female of that species. I loved his little bits of business and the way he always avoided the obvious."

Joseph Cotten (*Shadow of a Doubt*): "Hitch, in his later years, thought this the best of his films, and it is certainly mentioned to me as often as *Citizen Kane* and *The Third Man.*"

Hume Cronyn (*Shadow of a Doubt, Lifeboat;* adaptations: *Rope, Under Capricorn*): "He thought in images. The story was to be pictorially revealed, not just told; and he brought together the gifts of art director and cutter in the telling."

Tallulah Bankhead (*Lifeboat*): "Mr. Hitchcock is the largest director alive. For all I know, he may be the best. He has the equipment for his job. He learned it the hard way, through trial and error."

Ingrid Bergman (*Spellbound, Notorious, Under Capricorn*): Referring to Hitchcock's long takes on *Under Capricorn:* "How I hate this new technique of his. How I suffer and loathe every minute on the set."

"Every actor who has worked with Hitchcock would like to work with him again."

"Alfred Hitchcock is an adorable genius."

Gregory Peck (*Spellbound, The Paradine Case*): "During *Spellbound*, Hitchcock, weighing at three-hundred, kept up a running patter of suggestive remarks directed at Ingrid. English-schoolboy stuff from the master of suspense."

Cary Grant (*Suspicion, Notorious, To Catch a Thief, North by Northwest*): "He has his picture all finished before we even arrive."

Referring to *North by Northwest:* "We've already done a third of the picture, and I still can't make head or tail of it. I don't understand what's going on, and I doubt if anyone will."

"He couldn't have been a nicer fellow. I whistled coming to work on his films."

James Stewart (*Rope, Rear Window, The Man Who Knew Too Much, Vertigo*):
"Hitchcock believes that if you sit down with an actor and analyze a scene, you run the danger that the actor will act that scene with his head rather than his heart or guts."

"Hitchcock's life is as well planned as his movies."

"When you work with Hitch, you don't try to do a scene two ways. You do it one way. His."

Stewart declared when Hitchcock died: "I have lost a great friend, and the world has lost one of its finest directing talents. Alfred Hitchcock has made a tremendous contribution to the art of motion pictures and has been a source of joy to people all over the world."

Marlene Dietrich (*Stage Fright*): "What most impressed me about Hitchcock was his calm authority, his ability to give orders without being taken for a dictator. Hitchcock, effortlessly, never failed to captivate, to explain, to rule, to teach, to enchant. Yet, at the bottom, he was reserved. Like many geniuses, he didn't like being idolized."

Jane Wyman (*Stage Fright*): "He looks like a little tubby pixie."

Farley Granger (*Rope, Strangers on a Train*): "I remember seeing him sitting in his chair beside the set on the second day of shooting, and he looked very down. And I said, 'Hitch, what's the matter?' and he said, 'Oh, I'm so bored....I've done it all. Now all I have to do is tell you where to go and tell the camera where to go.'"

Montgomery Clift (*I Confess*): "Hitchcock still gets purple in the face when he hears my name."

Grace Kelly (*Dial M for Murder, Rear Window, To Catch a Thief*): "Working with Hitchcock was a tremendous experience and a very enriching one. As an actor, I learned a tremendous amount about motion picture making. He gave me a great deal of confidence in myself."

"I have such affection for him and his wife that he can do no wrong."

Doris Day (*The Man Who Knew Too Much*): "Although he had verbally communicated very little to me, somehow, by some mystical process, I had learned some important things about Hitchcock moviemaking that were to serve me as well in the future. Certainly, a lesson about confidence."

Kim Novak (*Vertigo*): "It was a great thrill working with him, and I learned a lot, but I was disappointed when he wouldn't discuss my characters with me...but that's the way he was."

James Mason (*North by Northwest*): "You can see from the way he uses actors that he sees them as animated props."

Martin Landau (*North by Northwest*): "Hitchcock had worked with Grant a lot, and so they were naturally close, whereas I think James Mason felt rather left out and suddenly realized he'd reached some kind of turning point."

Eva Marie Saint (*North by Northwest*): "Mr. Hitchcock deserves the credit for changing my image. Frankly, up to that time I would have never thought of myself as a woman of mystery."

America: The Later Years

Janet Leigh (*Psycho*):
"I'm a movie fan, so it only makes sense that I'm a Hitchcock fan! Each time I saw a film by him, I said, 'I want to work one day with this man.' All of his films are classics to me."

"I had met him at functions previously to *Psycho,* and he was always very charming and funny. What I had heard about him working was his camera expertise and the detailed preproduction he had on all his films. I had heard that he didn't have a great deal of respect for actors, which is a rumor that I found not to be true."

"I was not apprehensive about anything. But on the other hand, it is true that I was in a bit of a state of shock just because of working with such an important director, whom I highly respected."

"To me, *Psycho* was a big comedy. Had to be." —Hitchcock.

From left: Anthony Perkins, Vera Miles, Alfred Hitchcock, Janet Leigh, and John Gavin in *Psycho*.

John Gavin, Alfred Hitchcock, and Janet Leigh on the set of *Psycho*.

"John Gavin was a little bit too reserved in the opening scene so Hitchcock pulled me on the side and said: 'Janet, my girl, you've gotta get this guy a little hot.'" —Janet Leigh.

Hitchcock on the set of *Psycho* with his wife, Alma, and his daughter, Patricia.

"When I gave birth to our only child, Pat, I had a relatively easy time of it, but Hitch suffered such panic-pains, he might as well have changed places with me." —Alma Reville-Hitchcock.

"He was absolutely meticulous in his planning, which is how he could build up suspense in his films. It was like choreography in a dance. This method also allowed him to do inexpensive films."

"He prepared himself so well because he literally edited the film in his camera. After he left the picture, the studio could not come in and reedit his movie differently because it was all done during the shooting!"

"He was absolute about his camera and his camera moves, and I believe he had earned that right."

"He gave me total autonomy as long as I stayed in his frame of work."

"He chose the dummy of Mrs. Bates according to my scream. I would come back from lunch and that . . . that thing would be sitting in my dressing room! Hitchcock played that joke on me each time he would come up with a new version of Mrs. Bates!"

"John Gavin was a little bit too reserved in the opening scene, so Hitchcock pulled me to the side and said: 'Janet, my girl, you've gotta get this guy a little hot.'"

"At a premiere, there was an announcer who called in the cars for the celebrities. When the poor man saw Hitchcock, he became nervous and screamed: 'Mr. Hitchcar's cock!'"

Anthony Perkins (*Psycho*): "We had fun making it—never realizing the impact it would have."

Tippi Hedren (*The Birds; Marnie*): "I greatly honor Hitchcock and admire his talent."

Jessica Tandy (*The Birds*): "It's the first time I've ever been upstaged by two-thousand actors at once."

Veronica Cartwright (*The Birds*): "I had heard that Hitchcock didn't like kids. It was just a rumor, and I must say that he was always very nice and kind with me. I turned thirteen on the set, and he threw a huge surprise party."

Sean Connery (*Marnie*): "I had a great time with Hitchcock. He tells you on the set what moves he wants. The only major direction he gave me was when I was listening to what somebody else was saying in a scene and he pointed that I was listening with my mouth open—as I often do—and he thought it would look better shut."

John Forsythe (*The Trouble With Harry; Topaz*): "He's a formidable person. He's a story-minded little man, an austere figure, and actors are frightened of him."

Paul Newman (*Torn Curtain*): "Well, I think I could have hit it off with Hitchcock if the script had been better. That was the main problem. It was not a lack of communication or a lack of respect. The only thing that constantly stood in our way was the script."

Bruce Dern (*Family Plot*): "When he wants the audience emotionally moved, the camera moves."

Marlon Brando (who never made a film with Hitchcock): "John Ford would never have me in a picture because he directs from the director's point of view, not the actor's. . . . Alfred Hitchcock is another. He tells the same story over and over again, not from the human point of view but from the point of view of camera angles."

What Others Said About Hitch

Alma Reville-Hitchcock: "When I gave birth to our only child, Pat, I had a relatively easy time of it, but Hitch suffered such panic pains, he might as well have changed places with me."

"He can't stand the idea of facing the unexpected, and he becomes downright ill if you keep him in suspense."

"Frankly, Hitch feels that suspense is not psychologically or physically healthy for him."

"My husband believes that suspense is great for other people—but not for Alfred Hitchcock."

"People who have worked with Hitch describe him as the placid, nerveless type, but they don't realize that beneath his cherubic-like surface there is a deep pool of emotion."

"Hitch's mind is as balanced and as orderly as his personal habits."

"Hitch is extremely devoted to his grandchildren, but I think he is secretly glad there are no more than three."

"Hitch said I had—well, I don't know what to call it—a certain quality, a certain flip of the head, for example, that he liked. He compared it to the Grace Kelly quality."

Patricia Hitchcock: "My father belongs to that hardy group that plays practical jokes as a rough and spirited game."

And, in alphabetical order:

Saul Bass (pictorial consultant on *Psycho;* title designer on

Vertigo, North by Northwest, and *Psycho*): "I loved Hitch. I was still quite young when I first worked for him. He was a great patron, very encouraging and supportive. Working with him was like taking a film course."

Charles Bennett, screenwriter (*Blackmail, The Man Who Knew Too Much, The 39 Steps, Secret Agent, Sabotage, Young and Innocent, Foreign Correspondent*): "He hated writers. He thought writers were a very low form of life."

"I'll tell you the wonderful thing about Hitch is that he came up with great ideas, but too often, as a writer, you found out that his ideas just couldn't be used in the story."

"I think Hitch was a wonderful director. I could never underrate Hitch as a director. But he was not a writer. He was a brilliant director, and there's no part in any picture he made, woman or man, that Hitch couldn't have played himself. Sounds silly, but it's true."

Ingmar Bergman, director: "Thanks to Hitchcock, particularly, I'd long been intrigued by shooting long sequences in difficult and cramped circumstances, weeding out everything irrelevant—quite simply, in making things hard to myself."

Peter Bogdanovich, director: "I judged myself by the directors I admire. Hawks, Lubitsch, Keaton, Welles, Ford, and Hitchcock."

Raymond Chandler, writer (*Strangers on a Train*): "Hitchcock is a rather special kind of director. He is always ready to sacrifice dramatic logic (insofar as it exists) for the sake of a camera effect or mood effect."

Michael Crichton, writer/director: "*To Catch a Thief* was the first Hitchcock film I ever saw. I was about twelve. I don't think I had ever seen Cary Grant or Grace Kelly before. It was the most wonderful world. Sexy and romantic and dramatic and set in the Riviera. It made a great impression on me."

George Cukor, director: "I like Hitchcock—I think that he is highly original. He is a very talented man. He left his mark. His name only means mystery. It is synonymous to suspense. His name means something."

John Frankenheimer, director: "Any American director who says he hasn't been influenced by him is out of his mind."

William Friedkin, director: "He was with an entourage and put out his hand, which was kind of limp, and he said, 'Ah, Mr. Friedkin, I see you're not wearing a tie.' I thought he was kidding, and I said, 'No, that's right, I'm not wearing a tie.' 'Usually our directors wear ties.'"

Samuel Fuller, director: "Hitchcock...I liked *The 39 Steps*. I am not crazy about Hitchcock, and I haven's seen many of his films. His movies are light and entertaining, but I don't get anything out of them."

William Goldman, writer: "I think the last two decades of Hitchcock's career were a great waste and sadness. He was technically as skillful as ever. But he had become encased in praise, inured to any criticism. Hitchcock himself had become the man who knew too much. So yes, I think the auteur theory ruined him—or at least his belief in it."

Edith Head, costume designer:
"I just had to be sure that what I did pleased Hitch. He was very specific about costumes for his leading ladies. He spoke a designer's language, even though he didn't know the first thing about clothes. He specified colors in the script if they

were important. If he wanted a skirt that brushed a desk as a woman walked by, he spelled that out, too."

"Even in a brief conversation, Hitch could communicate complex idea."

"Loyalty was extremely important to Alfred Hitchcock. He was as loyal to his craftsmen as he expected them to be to him."

Ben Hecht, screenwriter (*Spellbound, Notorious*) (referring to the dialogue in *Notorious* between Cary Grant and Ingrid Bergman as they kiss while talking about dinner): "I don't get all this talk about chicken!"

Bernard Herrmann, music composer (*The Trouble With Harry, The Man Who Knew Too Much, The Wrong Man, Vertigo, North by Northwest, Psycho, Marnie.* Sound consultant on *The Birds.* Fired from *Torn Curtain*):
"Many directors can make one or two good movies, but how many can make fifty great ones like Hitchcock?"

"He is essentially a puritan. Yet it's the puritanical artist that achieves real sexual expression, because he conveys his ideas poetically through atmosphere."

"Hitch only finishes a picture sixty percent. I have to finish it for him."

Elia Kazan, director: "Hitchcock relied on his camera angles and his montage (the juxtaposition of short lengths of film) to do what onstage we relied on the actors for."

Stephen King, writer (referring to *Psycho*): "Here is a movie where blood was kept to a minimum and terror was kept to a maximum."

C. A. Lejeune, a British critic: "On the set, he's a sadist. He respects nobody's feelings; but everybody respects him."

Henry Mancini, music composer (who lost his job on *Frenzy*): "Apart from the film, I found Mr. Hitchcock to be a gracious and generous man."

Cecil B. DeMille, director: "Part of the fun of seeing a Hitchcock picture is in spotting that distinguished director in the corner of some crowd scene, buying a newspaper or lighting a cigar or hurrying through a crowd to catch a train. It is fun for Mr. Hitchcock, too."

Brian De Palma, director: "Here's one of the few directors who advanced the form of cinema. Anybody who knows anything about film grammar cannot help but be snowed under by Hitchcock."

Michael Powell, director/screenwriter/producer (still photographer on Hitchcock's *Blackmail*): "He thought he could do everything. It took him some years to learn from his mistakes. But in the making of them, and in the years that followed, he was the most inventive, mischievous, inspiring hobgoblin in movies, and movies were all the better for him. He also loved telling filthy stories. The filthier, the better."

Otto Preminger, director: "I think that Hitch is a master in his own genre. I would never try to imitate him. Hitch has a knack of telling a story."

Miklos Rozsa, music composer (*Spellbound*): "With Alfred Hitchcock there had been no partnership at all: we had never really clicked. I disliked his overbearing attitude, and he, I presume, was uninterested in my music, since he never came to the recording sessions and never bothered to congratulate me on winning the Oscar. (Even Selznick [who produced *Spellbound*] had had the courtesy to send me a telegram.)"

"The late Alfred Hitchcock asked me at the time how long it would take to write the music for *Spellbound*. I stipulated six weeks. 'Six weeks,' he thundered. 'I shot the whole picture in that time!' 'Very possible,' I replied, 'but how long did it take you and Ben Hecht to write the screenplay?' He just grunted."

Andrew Sarris, critic: "His reputation has suffered from the fact that he has given audiences more pleasure that is permissible in serious cinema."

David O. Selznick, producer: "Not a bad guy . . . although not exactly a man to go camping with."

Joseph Stefano, screenwriter (*Psycho*): "I wasn't at all surprised that *Psycho* was a fantastic hit. Hitch had no sense of how it was going to affect his future films."

François Truffaut, director and author of *Hitchcock/Truffaut:* "I have loved Hitchcock every step of the way. I loved him when I was just a film buff. I loved him when I became a critic, and my admiration continued when I started directing films."

"When I direct a movie, I realize that if I'm having problems with a scene, I always find a solution if I think of Hitchcock."

Walter Wanger, producer (*Foreign Correspondent*): "He arrives in the morning, is punctual on the stage, makes a careful check of his script scenes before he starts, and while he drinks a cup of black coffee, directs the first setup in the minutest detail."

Orson Welles, director/writer/producer/actor: "Hitchcock is an incredible director."

To Catch a Film

Generally, movie studios market their films around the actors who star in them and are responsible for educating audiences as to who is in front of the camera, not who is behind it. Alfred Hitchcock, however, was an exception to this rule.

Very early on in his career, Hitchcock became the star of his movies; audiences were going to see "the new Hitchcock film." The ad campaigns and trailers for his films always referred to Hitchcock; he was the guarantee to the audience that the movie was good. Hitchcock was able to maintain this power throughout his career; audiences were familiar with him because of his cameo appearances and, of course, because of his TV show "Alfred Hitchcock Presents," which became popular in the late fifties. Hitchcock himself appeared in his trailers and on the posters of his films.

Hitchcock's campaigns became especially creative with *Psycho*. In 1956, Hitchcock saw the French classic thriller *Les Diaboliques* by Henri-Georges Clouzot. A title card at the end of the film said: "Don't be diabolical yourself. Don't spoil the ending for your friends by telling them what you've just seen. On their behalf, thank you!" The *Psycho* ad campaign said: "By the way, after you see the picture, please don't give away the ending. It's the only one we have!"

A Hitchcock film was always an event, and the excitment, the suspense, the thrills, began long before the audience walked into the theater.

Ad Campaigns

Sabotage

"Sylvia Sidney tells Oscar Homolka, her screen husband in SABOTAGE, that dinner is served. For your dinner, remember to buy your meat from Bull & Co."

"Sylvia Sidney has well-groomed hair. Why not copy her example and visit Maison Louis Coiffeur?"

Suspicion

"Suspense that mounts with every embrace! A story of love...under the threat of murder!"

"Who was this man she married?
Cheat? Murderer? Wastrel? Deceiver?"

"These three make history! Cary Grant as the playboy-husband intent on riches at any cost! Joan Fontaine, REBECCA's star, as the bride in terror of the man she loved! Alfred Hitchcock directing his masterpiece of suspense!"

"She was made to live for him...to die for him—Yet she did not really know him!"

"Two great stars and a great director bring you the drama of a bride's doubting heart!"

"Is he just gay and irresponsible?
Has he given up the women of his past?

Is he the cheat and fraud they say?
Would he murder to get money... To get my money?"

Notorious

"Notorious woman of affairs! Adventurous man of the world!
The boldest masquerade two lovers ever dared!"

"Would you force the woman you love to marry the man she
hated? Would you marry a traitor to prove yourself a patriot?
Why did he demand she pay a daring price (to her love)?"

"Why must I scorn her... yet I can't resist her kisses?
Why must I have only stolen kisses with the man I love?"

"Why was this key more dangerous than any other killer's
knife?"

Strangers on a Train

"You'll be in the grip of love's strangest trip! It begins with the
shriek of a train whistle and ends with shrieking excitment!
Young America's idol—a good-looking stranger in search of
sensation—and a girl in love. These are the people around
whom Alfred Hitchcock spins his wonderful web of suspense
and surprise. Warner Bros. bring a pounding new tempo to
motion picture entertainment. It's off the beaten track!"

To Catch a Thief

"It's Hitchcock! It's Monte Carlo! It's Cary Grant and Grace
Kelly! It's a web of romance and suspense that spins you from
delight to danger—then spirals to an explosive climax on the
fabulous Riviera!"

"... For a moment he forgets he's a thief—and she forgets she's
a lady! It's the year's danger sensation with the love scenes of
the century! When they meet in Monte Carlo your emotions
are in for a pounding!"

"So intense you'll feel your own heart flaming! The burning promise of her lips...The flashing diamonds at her throat...These were the baits she used...to catch a thief in Monte Carlo!"

The Wrong Man
"For the first time Alfred Hitchcock goes to real life for his thrills! It's all true and all suspense—the all-'round biggest Hitchcock hit ever to hit the screen! Warner Bros. present Henry Fonda and Vera Miles and the exciting city of New York in Alfred Hitchcock's THE WRONG MAN."

"Somewhere...Somewhere...There must be the right man!"

"25 steps down into a subway—and for the first time he doesn't come home that night!"

"Challenge! If you don't believe that this weird and unusual story actually happened, see the records of Queens County Court, N.Y. April 21, 1953. Indictment # 271/53. 'The Balestrero Case.'"

North by Northwest
"Here a spy...There a spy...Everywhere a spy!"

"Only Cary Grant and Alfred Hitchcock ever gave you so much suspense in so many directions. So we brought it back."

"The spies come at you from all directions. Dodge a killer plane...Meet a beautiful spy...Play with some beautiful gadgets...Don't drop your microfilm...Run from the cops, killers, secret agents, beautiful women...And see if you can do all this without wrinkling your suit!"

"From the killer plane in the cornfield to the cliff-hanger on George Washington's nose, it's suspense in every direction."

"The Master of Suspense weaves his greatest tale!...about a secret that nobody knew...A man who never existed...And a breathless chase to the summit of suspense."

"2,000 miles they fled, NORTH BY NORTHWEST...The fastest way to the summit of suspense."

"A train may be an old-fashioned way to travel, but an upper berth can be a lovely way to go—when it's your time to go!"

"To make love...or be killed! Her lips promised one...Her gun the other, and the only thing that could save him now was a man who never existed."

"The lipstick on his collar marked him for murder!...Now he must run for his life—searching for a man who never was...A secret he could never know...And a girl he had once met in an upper berth!"

"We'll never tell what happens to Cary Grant, but we'll not keep your secret, Mr. Hitchcock! We know that making the motion picture *North by Northwest* has been your secret ambition for many years. We know its breathless chase, from the U.N. building in New York to the great stone faces of Mt. Rushmore, has never been rivalled in screen excitment. We are proud to have shared in its making...and believe that audiences everywhere will agree—it's your best, Mr. Hitchcock."—M-G-M Studios.

Psycho
"This film has so many twists and turns, it would be unfair to reveal them...and it would be especially unfair to reveal the surprise ending."

"We won't allow you to cheat yourself! You must see *Psycho* from beginning to end to enjoy it fully. Therefore, do not expect to be admitted into the theatre after the start of each performance of the picture. We say no one—and we mean no one—not even the manager's brother, the President of the United States, or the Queen of England (God bless her)!— Alfred Hitchcock."

"Surely you do not have your meat course after your dessert at dinner. You will therefore understand why we are so insistent that you enjoy *Psycho* from start to finish, exactly as we intended that it be served.—Alfred Hitchcock."

"*Psycho* is most enjoyable when viewed beginning at the beginning and proceeding to the end. I realize this is a revolutionary concept but we have discovered that *Psycho* is unlike most motion pictures and does not improve when run backwards. Therefore, we will not allow you to cheat yourself. So do not expect to be admitted to the theatre after the start of each performance of the picture.—Alfred Hitchcock."

"The entire objective of this extraordinary policy, of course, is to help you enjoy *Psycho* more.—Alfred Hitchcock."

Recordings for theater lobbies:
"This is Alfred Hitchcock...We trust that the presence of a special policeman throughout the current engagement of *Psycho* will not prove annoying or frightening. Personally, they scare me to death. Actually, he merely represents the theatre management, who have been instructed to make certain that no one is seated after the picture begins."

"This is Alfred Hitchcock...Having lived with *Psycho* since it was a gleam in my camera's eye, I now exercise my parental rights in revealing a number of significant facts about this well-eh-uh slightly extraordinary entertainment. I must warn you that *Psycho* was designed to be as terrifying as possible.

Do not, however, heed the false rumor that it will frighten the moviegoer speechless. We do want your friends to come too."

The Birds
"THE BIRDS is coming!"

"People do enjoy being scared, you know—as long as they know they will be safe at the end of the experience. With THE BIRDS, we will fulfill their enjoyment. But it will all be up there on the screen. We promise not to turn a single bird loose in any theatre."

"Hitchcock's THE BIRDS is exciting and absolutely terrifying. They attack women and kill other people."

"Nothing you have ever witnessed before has prepared you for such sheer stabbing shock!"

Radio Spot: [SOUND OF CUCKOO CLOCK]. Hitchcock: "The opinions expressed are not necessarily those of the management. This is Alfred Hitchcock bringing you the correct time. It is now high time you saw THE BIRDS. Because of the unusual nature of this film, THE BIRDS should be seen from the beginning. Those of you who read magazines from back to front will consider this most peculiar, but please permit us this whim. It's for your own good." [SOUND OF CUCKOO CLOCK]

Recording for theater lobbies: "How do you do. This is Alfred Hitchcock; that is, the spirit of Alfred Hitchcock. It was felt that in a lobby as crowded as this one, what was needed was more spirit than flesh. I wish to thank you for your patience and splendid cooperation. However, I know you have enjoyed standing around like this. In fact, there are some who say that waiting in line is the best part of the evening.

We do this, of course, not as part of the nation's emphasis

on physical fitness but because we think you can enjoy THE BIRDS more if you see it from the start to finish instead of vice versa. As for THE BIRDS, I am sure they are as eager to see you as you are to see them. We make them wait on line too."

Marnie

"Only Alfred Hitchcock could have created such a suspense-ful sex mystery as MARNIE...she's a thief...liar...cheat, yet more woman than man can resist!"

"Only Alfred Hitchcock could have created a woman—so mysterious—so fascinating—so dangerous as MARNIE."

"From Alfred Hitchcock with sex and suspense."

"On MARNIE's wedding night he discovered every secret about her...except one!"

"Alfred Hitchcock's love stories start where others fail to go!"

"Would his touch end MARNIE's unnatural fears...or start them again?"

"Thief...Liar...Cheat...She was all of these...And he knew it! Yet he loved her...Married her. What was the riddle of MARNIE?"

"The more he loved her...The more she hated him...For trying to unravel her secret!"

"Is Alfred Hitchcock's MARNIE: a sex story? A mystery? A detective story? A romance? A story of a thief? A love story? YES AND MORE!"

"You don't love me. I'm just something you caught. You think I'm some kind of animal you've trapped."

"That's right, you are and I caught something really wild this time, haven't I? I've tracked you and caught you and by god I'm going to keep you!"

Tippi Hedren and Sean Connery in *Marnie*.

"Held over! You must see Alfred Hitchcock's MARNIE twice to really enjoy the suspenseful love story."

"Why MARNIE did what she did unfolds in the last 10 minutes...So NO one will be admitted!"

Radio spot:
Alfred Hitchcock: "Do you have money problems? Are you hopelessly in debt? Wondering where the next dollar is coming from? This is Alfred Hitchcock suggesting: Why don't you do as MARNIE does? Consolidate all your debts and then wipe them out in one enormous heist. There are dangers, of course. MARNIE seemed to enjoy taking the money. Robbery followed robbery. And then she met a man...but I am telling you too much. If you are interested in this questionable method of achieving solvency, you will have to see MARNIE. MARNIE is my latest motion picture. Don't stage another robbery until you see MARNIE."

Alfred Hitchcock: "I wouldn't trust MARNIE any farther than I could throw Alfred Hitchcock. This is a terrible thing to say about a lady. But then—MARNIE is no lady. Personally, I wouldn't have a thing to do with her. However, if you would, you'll find her at your favorite theatre."

Trailers

Rebecca (trailer for the rerelease of the film)
"Announcing the return of the most glamorous motion picture ever made. David O. Selznick and Alfred Hitchcock bring you the grand slam prize winner that made motion picture history. Winner of the Academy Award, voted by America's critics as the best picture of the year. And now as a result of a national pole, winning new honors as audiences throughout the coun-

try vote to see it again. The Selznick's Studios successor to GONE WITH THE WIND, REBECCA!"

Suspicion

Joan Fontaine addressed the audience over clips of the film: "There was something strange about John Aysgarth. I knew it long before I married him... something you couldn't put your finger on, and yet you were always conscious of it. Conscious of something vague, restless, frightening." Joan Fontaine concluded at the end of the trailer: "These are the facts, the evidence before the crime. I wanted you to know in case I met a violent end...."

Saboteur

Robert Cummings addressed the audience over clips of the film: "I'm Barry Kane, American. Right now, I'm a fugitive. A couple of days ago, I was an aircraft worker. Then something happened. Something that could only happen in times like these.... My best friend died in that fire. The authorities questioned everybody. I told them what I knew. I even offered to help. But it was no good; they wouldn't believe me...."

Shadow of a Doubt (trailer for the rerelease of the film)

"So great, the world can never forget it. So thrilling, it had to be brought back. Teresa Wright, Joseph Cotten, in a masterpiece of mystery and suspense...Alfred Hitchcock's SHADOW OF A DOUBT. Terror warning her to kill...or be killed..."

Spellbound

Freeze frame on Hitchcock's cameo appearance in the film, coming out of an elevator. Voice off: "Don't forget this man. He has plenty to do with the terrifying mystery that causes this glamorous woman (Ingrid Bergman) to risk her life and reputation in a reckless experiment...A woman who, because of her consuming love for this man (Gregory Peck), gambles everything to unlock the fearful secret in his heart. What insidious meaning did he read into the markings on the tablecloth? Why, even when he held his sweetheart in his arms, did he gaze in fear at the dark lines of her robe. These are some of the clues in the picture which bears Hollywood's most distinguished mark of quality: A Selznick International Picture. SPELLBOUND..."

The trailer concluded over Hitchcock's cameo appearance: "We told you not to forget this man. He is Alfred Hitchcock, the famous director, whom you're not likely to forget after you see SPELLBOUND!"

Notorious

"A notorious woman of affairs! An adventurous man of the world! They meet...and fall in love! Recklessly! Daringly! Dangerously! Cary Grant, Ingrid Bergman have thrilled you before...but never like this! Together for the first time! In Alfred Hitchcock's NOTORIOUS! A fateful fascination charged with mounting danger! A mad adventure fraught with bold intrigue! Daringly directed by that master of suspense Alfred Hitchcock."

Rope

The trailer opened with a scene that's not in the film. It showed David Kentley (Dick Hogan) and his girlfriend, Janet (Joan Chandler), in Central Park discussing their relationship. David leaves, telling Janet he would see her later at a party. James Stewart then addressed the audience: "That's the last time she ever saw him alive, and that's the last time you'll ever see him alive. What happened to David Kentley changed my life completely, and the lives of seven others..."

Title cards announced: "Alfred Hitchcock's first Technicolor picture. ROPE. Alfred Hitchcock's most startling adventure in suspense. ROPE. Alfred Hitchcock tells a story you will never forget."

Dial M for Murder

The trailer showed a hand picking up a phone: "Alfred Hitchcock's masterpiece of mystery and melodrama. DIAL M FOR MURDER, from the stage play that held two continents spellbound with suspense! Listen to the voice of critics' praise: *The New York Times* called it 'King Lear with excitment.' *The Detroit News* said: 'It's the best crime play in years!' *The London Daily Mail* headlined 'A murder thriller with a difference.' *The New York Daily Mirror* wrote: 'It holds your attention like a vice.'" The trailer concluded: "An experience in excitment that will twist your emotions into tight knots! DIAL M FOR MURDER. A direct line to high tension drama you'll never forget!"

Rear Window

"This is the scene of the crime. A crime of passion filmed in a way you have never seen before and as no one else would dare attempt but the screen's master of suspense, Alfred Hitchcock." The trailer showed James Stewart's neighbors; the actor then addressed the audience: "Those are just a few of my neighbors. First I watched them just to kill time, but then I couldn't take my eyes off them, just as you won't be able to....And you won't be able to take your eyes off the glorious beauty of Grace Kelly, who shares the heart and curiosity of James Stewart in this story of a romance shadowed by the terror of a horrifying secret. REAR WINDOW."

The Trouble With Harry

Voice off: a man lying in a field: "Something's wrong here. This man is not sleeping. He is dead and Alfred Hitchcock did it...in a completely different way, for you've never seen anything like THE TROUBLE WITH HARRY."

The trailer concluded: "You won't stop laughing at THE TROUBLE WITH HARRY, Alfred Hitchcock's comedy about a body."

The Man Who Knew Too Much (1956)
"Alfred Hitchcock strikes the highest note of suspense the screen has yet achieved! THE MAN WHO KNEW TOO MUCH." James Stewart then addressed the audience: "You're right. That was a gunshot you heard. That was the signal that brought all the trouble out in the open. It's a scene from our new picture THE MAN WHO KNEW TOO MUCH. As you know, Alfred Hitchcock has a uncanning knack for coming up with the unusual in entertainment. Well, THE MAN WHO KNEW TOO MUCH can certainly be put in that category...."

The Wrong Man
In THE WRONG MAN, Alfred Hitchcock appeared in person at the beginning of the film. This was almost like showing a trailer before the movie began: "This is Aflred Hitchcock speaking. In the past, I have given you many kinds of suspense pictures, but this time, I would like you to see a different one. The difference lies in the fact that this is a true story, every word of it. And yet it contains elements that are stranger than all the fiction that has gone into many of the thrillers that I've made before."

Vertigo
"VERTIGO...A feeling of dizziness...A swimming in the head...Figuratively a state in which all things seem to be engulfed in a whirlpool of terror. As created by Alfred Hitchcock in a story that gives new meaning to the word suspense...."

The trailer concluded: "James Stewart as you've never seen him before. Kim Novak playing two amazing roles. Only

"When I was a very young child—oh, about four years old—my father sent me to the police station with a note. I assume I was being punished. The police locked me in a cell for about five minutes, saying, 'this is what we do to naughty boys.' I've been literally terrified of policemen ever since." —Alfred Hitchcock.

Hitchcock could weave this tangled web of terror. VERTIGO."

Psycho

Voice off: "The fabulous Mr. Alfred Hitchcock is about to escort you on a tour of the location of his new motion picture PSYCHO." Hitchcock took the audience to the Bates Motel and to the Bates house, describing some of the key scenes that took place in the various locations. The trailer ended, of course, in the bathroom: "Well, uh, they cleaned all this up now. Big difference. You should have seen the blood. The whole...the whole place....Well, uh, it's too horrible to describe. Dreadful."

The Birds

Alfred Hitchcock, addressing the audience: "How do you do? My name is Alfred Hitchcock, and I would like to tell you about my forthcoming lecture. It is about the birds and their age-long relationship with man. It will be seen in theaters like this across the country...."

Marnie

Hitchcock, addressing the audience: "How do you do? I'm Alfred Hitchcock, and I would like to tell you about my latest motion picture, MARNIE, which will be coming to this theatre soon. MARNIE is a very difficult picture to classify. It is not PSYCHO, nor do we have a horde of birds flapping about and pecking at people willy-nilly. We do have two very interesting human specimens: a man and a woman. One might call MARNIE a sex mystery, that is, if one uses such words, but it is more than that...."

Frenzy

Hitchcock was seen floating on his back on the Thames River and addressing the audience: "I dare say, you are wondering why I'm floating around London like this. I am on the famous

Thames River investigating a murder. Rivers can be very sinister places, and in my new film *Frenzy*, this river, you may say, was the scene of a horrible crime."

Later, Hitchcock stood in front of a bag of potatoes: "Here is the scene of another horrible murder. This is the famous London wholesale fruit and vegetable market Covent Garden. Here you may buy the fruits of evil and the horrors of the vegetables. (As he opens the bag of potatoes, a woman's leg appears.) I've heard of a leg of lamb, a leg of chicken, but never of a leg of potatoes."

Last Words

I think somebody once said to me," Hitchcock declared, "what's your idea of happiness, and I said, a clear horizon, no clouds, no shadows, nothing." This remark is quite unexpected coming from someone who left behind him such a wealth of images. What Hitchcock might have meant here is that his idea of happiness is a white screen—but on which he could project his own images.

Hitchcock could only live one way, and that was through his films; he never stopped working. Movies were his life-support system. His movies in return became the life-support system of the film industry. Hitchcock was a great teacher only because he was forced to learn—and expand—an art that was still young when he himself began his directing career.

Truffaut said: "Hitchcock not only intensified life; he intensified cinema." This book hopefully proves that Hitchcock also intensified love, death, food even! So, next time you watch a Hitchcock film, don't forget to listen as well. Words also can be deceiving....

Filmography

Note to the reader: The dates indicate the year in which the films were released.

The British Years

Silent Films

NUMBER THIRTEEN (Wardour & F/1922) (unfinished)
Directed and produced by Alfred Hitchcock. Starring Clare Greet, Ernest Thesiger.

THE PLEASURE GARDEN (a Gainsborough-Emelka Picture/1925)
Directed by Alfred Hitchcock. Produced by Michael Balcon. Screenplay by Eliot Stannard, based on the novel by Oliver Sandys. Starring: Virginia Valli, Carmelita Geraghty, Miles Mander.

THE MOUNTAIN EAGLE (a Gainsborough-Emelka Picture/1927)
Directed by Alfred Hitchcock. Produced by Michael Balcon. Screenplay by Eliot Stannard. Starring: Bernard Goetzke, Nita Naldi, Malcolm Keen.

THE LODGER: A STORY OF THE LONDON FOG (a Gainsborough Picture/1927)
Directed by Alfred Hitchcock. Produced by Michael Balcon. Screenplay by Eliot Stannard, based on the novel *The Lodger* by Marie Belloc Lowndes. Starring: Ivor Novello, Malcolm Keen, June.

DOWNHILL (released in the U.S.A. as WHEN BOYS LEAVE HOME); a Gainsborough Picture/1927)
Directed by Alfred Hitchcock. Produced by Michael Balcon. Screenplay by Eliot Stannard, based on the play by David LeStrange (pseudonym for Ivor Novello and Constance Collier). Starring: Ivor Novello, Robin Irvine, Lillian Braithwaite.

EASY VIRTUE (a Gainsborough Picture/1927)
Directed by Alfred Hitchcock. Produced by Michael Balcon. Screenplay by Eliot Stannard, based on the play by Noel Coward. Starring: Isabel Jeans, Ian Hunter, Robin Irvine.

THE RING (a British International Picture/1927)
Directed by Alfred Hitchcock. Produced by John Maxwell. Screenplay by Alfred Hitchcock. Starring: Carl Brisson, Lillian Hall-Davis, Ian Hutner.

THE FARMER'S WIFE (a British International Picture/1928)
Directed by Alfred Hitchcock. Produced by John Maxwell. Screenplay by Alfred Hitchcock, based on the play by Eden Philpotts. Starring: Jameson Thomas, Lillian Hall-Davis, Gordon Harker.

CHAMPAGNE (a British International Picture/1928)
Directed by Alfred Hitchcock. Produced by John Maxwell. Adaptation by Alfred Hitchcock, based on an original story by Walter C. Mycroft. Starring: Betty Balfour, Jean Bradin, Ferdinand Von Alten

THE MANXMAN (a British International Picture/1929)
Directed by Alfred Hitchcock. Produced by John Maxwell. Screenplay by Eliot Stannard, based on the novel by Hall Caine. Starring: Carol Brisson, Malcolm Keen, Anny Ondra.

Sound Films

BLACKMAIL (a British International Picture/1929)
Directed by Alfred Hitchcock. Produced by John Maxwell. Screenplay by Alfred Hitchcock, based on the play by Charles Bennett. Dialogue by Benn Levy. Starring: Anny Ondra (voice: Joan Barry), John Longden, Donald Calthrop, Cyril Ritchard.

ELSTREE CALLING (a British International Picture/1930)
Directed by Alfred Hitchcock, André Charlot, Jack Hulbert, Adrian Bunel, and Paul Murray. Screenplay by Adrian Bunel, Walter C. Mycroft, and Val Valentine. Starring: Tommy Handley, Jack Hulbert, Anna May Wong, Donald Calthrop.

JUNO AND THE PAYCOCK (a British International Picture/1930)
Directed by Alfred Hitchcock. Produced by John Maxwell. Adaptation by Alfred Hitchcock and Alma Reville, based on the play by Sean O'Casey. Starring: Sara Allgood, Edward Chapman, Maire O'Neill.

MURDER! (a British International Picture/1930)
Directed by Alfred Hitchcock. Produced by John Maxwell. Adaptation by Alfred Hitchcock and Walter Mycroft, based on the novel and the play *Enter Sir John* by Clemence Dane and Helen Simpson. Starring: Norah Baring, Herbert Marshall, Miles Mander.

THE SKIN GAME (a British International Picture/1931)
Directed by Alfred Hitchcock. Produced by John Maxwell. Screenplay by Alma Reville, based on the play by John Galsworthy. Starring: C. V. France, Helen Haye, Edmund Gwenn.

NUMBER SEVENTEEN (a British International Picture/1932)
Directed by Alfred Hitchcock. Produced by John Maxwell. Screenplay by Alma Reville, Alfred Hitchcock, and Rodney Ackland, based on the play by J. Jefferson Fargeon. Starring: Leon M. Lion, Anne Grey, John Stuart.

RICH AND STRANGE (released in the U.S.A. as EAST OF SHANGHAI; a British International Picture/1932)
Directed by Alfred Hitchcock. Produced by John Maxwell. Adaptation by Alfred Hitchcock. Screenplay by Alma Reville. Additional dialogue: Val Valentine. Starring: Henry Kendall, Joan Barry, Percy Marmont.

WALTZES FROM VIENNA (released in the U.S.A. as STRAUSS'S GREAT WALTZ; a Tom Arnold Productions/1933)
Directed by Alfred Hitchcock. Produced by Tom Arnold. Screenplay by Alma Reville and Guy Bolton, based on the play by Guy Bolton. Starring: Jessie Matthews, Esmond Knight, Edmund Gwenn.

THE MAN WHO KNEW TOO MUCH (a Gaumont-British Picture/1934)
Directed by Alfred Hitchcock. Produced by Michael Balcon.
Screenplay by Edwin Greenwood and A. R. Rawlinson, based on a
story by Charles Bennett and D. B. Wyndham Lewis. Additional
dialogue by Emlyn Williams. Starring: Leslie Banks, Edna Best,
Nova Pilbeam, Peter Lorre, Frank Vosper, Pierre Fresnay.

THE 39 STEPS (a Gaumont-British Picture/1935)
Directed by Alfred Hitchcock. Produced by Michael Balcon. Adap-
tation by Charles Bennett, based on the novel *The Thirty-Nine Steps*
by John Buchan. Dialogue by Ian Hay. Starring: Robert Donat,
Madeleine Carroll, Lucie Mannheim, Godfrey Tearle, John Laurie,
Peggy Ashcroft.

SECRET AGENT (a Gaumont-Picture/1936)
Directed by Alfred Hitchcock. Produced by Ivor Montagu.
Screenplay by Charles Bennett, from the play by Campbell Dixon,
based on stories by W. Somerset Maugham. Dialogue by Ian Hay and
Jesse Lasky, Jr. Starring: John Gielgud, Madeleine Carroll, Peter
Lorre.

SABOTAGE (released in the U.S.A. as THE WOMAN ALONE; a Gaumont-
British Picture/1936)
Directed by Alfred Hitchcock. Produced by Michael Balcon.
Screenplay by Charles Bennett, based on the novel *The Secret Agent*
by Joseph Conrad. Dialogue by Ian Hay and Helen Simpson.
Starring: Sylvia Sidney, Oscar Homolka, Desmond Tester, John
Loder, Joyce Barbour.

YOUNG AND INNOCENT (released in the U.S.A. as THE GIRL WAS
YOUNG; a Gaumont-British Picture/1938)
Directed by Alfred Hitchcock. Produced by Edward Black.
Screenplay by Charles Bennett, Edwin Greenwood, and Anthony
Armstrong, based on the novel *A Shilling for Candles* by Josephine
Tey. Dialogue by Gerald Savory. Starring: Nova Pilbeam, Derrick de
Marney, Percy Marmont, John Longden, George Curzon, Basil
Radford, Pamela Carme.

THE LADY VANISHES (a Gaumont-British Picture/1938)
Directed by Alfred Hitchcock. Produced by Edward Black.
Screenplay by Sidney Gilliat and Frank Lauder, based on the novel
The Wheel Spins by Ethel Lina White. Starring: Margaret Lock-

wood, Michael Redgrave, Dame May Whitty, Paul Lukas, Cecil Parker, Linden Travers, Naunton Wayne, Basil Radford.

JAMAICA INN (an Erich Pommer Production/1939)
Directed by Alfred Hitchcock. Produced by Erich Pommer. Screenplay by Sidney Giliat and Joan Harrison, based on the novel by Daphne du Maurier. Additional dialogue by J. B. Priestley. Starring: Charles Laughton, Maureen O'Hara, Leslie Banks.

The American Years

REBECCA (a Selznick International Picture/1940)
Directed by Alfred Hitchcock. Produced by David O. Selznick. Screenplay by Robert E. Sherwood and Joan Harrison, based on the novel by Daphne Du Maurier. Adaptation by Philip MacDonald and Michael Hogan. Starring: Laurence Olivier, Joan Fontaine, Judith Anderson, George Sanders, Florence Bates, Nigel Bruce, Gladys Cooper.

FOREIGN CORRESPONDENT (a Wanger Production. Distributed by United Artists/1940)
Directed by Alfred Hitchcock. Produced by Walter Wanger. Screenplay by Charles Bennett and Joan Harrison. Dialogue by James Hilton and Robert Benchley. Starring: Joel McCrea, Laraine Day, Herbert Marshall, George Sanders, Albert Basserman, Robert Benchley, Edmund Gwenn.

MR. AND MRS. SMITH (an RKO Radio Picture/1941)
Directed by Alfred Hitchcock. Produced by Harry E. Edington. Story and screenplay by Norman Krasna. Starring: Carole Lombard, Robert Montgomery, Gene Raymond.

SUSPICION (an RKO Radio Picture/1941)
Directed by Alfred Hitchcock. Produced by Harry E. Edington. Screenplay by Samson Raphaelson, Joan Harrison, and Alma Reville, based on the novel *Before the Facts* by Francis Isles. Starring: Joan Fontaine, Cary Grant, Sir Cedric Hardwicke, Dame May Whitty, Nigel Bruce, Auriol Lee, Leo G. Carroll, Heather Angel.

SABOTEUR (a Frank Lloyd Production for Universal Pictures/1942)
Directed by Alfred Hitchcock. Produced by Frank Lloyd.

Screenplay by Peter Viertel, Joan Harrison, and Dorothy Parker. Starring: Robert Cummings, Priscilla Lane, Otto Kruger, Alma Kruger, Norman Lloyd.

SHADOW OF A DOUBT (a Jack H. Skirball Production for Universal Pictures/1943)
Directed by Alfred Hitchcock. Produced by Jack H. Skirball. Screenplay by Thornton Wilder, Sally Benson, and Alma Reville, based on an original story by Gordon McDonell. Starring: Joseph Cotten, Teresa Wright, Macdonald Carey, Patricia Collinge, Henry Travers, Hume Cronyn, Edna May Wonacott, Charles Bates.

LIFEBOAT (a 20th Century-Fox Picture/1944)
Directed by Alfred Hitchcock. Produced by Kenneth Macgowan. Screenplay by Jo Swerling, based on a story by John Steinbeck. Starring: Tallulah Bankhead, John Hodiak, William Bendix, Hume Cronyn, Walter Slezak.

SPELLBOUND (a Selznick International Picture/1945)
Directed by Alfred Hitchcock. Produced by David O. Selznick. Screenplay by Ben Hecht, based on the novel *The House of Dr. Edwardes* by Francis Beeding. Adaptation by Angus MacPhail. Starring: Ingrid Bergman, Gregory Peck, Leo G. Carroll, Norman Lloyd, Michael Chekhov, John Emery.

NOTORIOUS (an RKO Radio Picture/1946)
Directed and produced by Alfred Hitchcock. Screenplay by Ben Hecht. Starring: Ingrid Bergman, Cary Grant, Claude Rains, Leopoldine Konstantin, Louis Calhern, Ivan Triesault.

THE PARADINE CASE (a David O. Selznick/Vanguard Film/1947)
Directed by Alfred Hitchcock. Produced by David O. Selznick. Screenplay by David O. Selznick, based on the novel by Robert Hichens. Adaptation by Alma Reville. Starring: Gregory Peck, Ann Todd, Valli, Charles Laughton, Louis Jourdan, Ethel Barrymore, Charles Coburn, Joan Tetzel, Leo G. Carroll.

ROPE (a Transatlantic Picture released by Warner Brothers/1948)
Directed by Alfred Hitchcock. Produced by Alfred Hitchcock and Sidney Bernstein. Adaptation by Hume Cronyn, based on the play by Patrick Hamilton. Screenplay by Arthur Laurents. Starring: James Stewart, John Dall, Farley Granger, Sir Cedric Hardwicke, Constance Collier, Joan Chandler.

UNDER CAPRICORN (a Transatlantic Picture released by Warner Brothers/1949)
Directed by Alfred Hitchcock. Produced by Alfred Hitchcock and Sidney Bernstein. Adaptation by Hume Cronyn. Screenplay by James Bridie, from the play by John Colton and Margaret Linden, based on the novel by Helen Simpson. Starring: Ingrid Bergman, Joseph Cotten, Michael Wilding, Margaret Leighton, Cecil Parker.

STAGE FRIGHT (a Warner Brothers-First National Picture production/1950)
Directed and produced by Alfred Hitchcock. Adaptation by Alma Reville. Screenplay by Whitfield Cook, based on the novel *Man Running* by Selwyn Jepson. Additional dialogue by James Bridie. Starring: Jane Wyman, Marlene Dietrich, Michael Wilding, Richard Todd, Alastair Sim, Sybil Thorndike, Patricia Hitchcock, Kay Walsh.

STRANGERS ON A TRAIN (a Warner Brothers-First National Picture production/1951)
Directed by Alfred Hitchcock. Produced by Alfred Hitchcock. Adaptation by Whitfield Cook. Screenplay by Raymond Chandler and Czenzi Ormonde, based on the novel by Patricia Highsmith. Starring Robert Walker, Farley Granger, Ruth Roman, Patricia Hitchcock, Laura Elliot, Leo G. Carroll, Marion Lorne.

I CONFESS (a Warner Brothers-First National Picture production/1953)
Directed and produced by Alfred Hitchcock. Screenplay by George Tabori and William Archibald, based on the novel *Nos Deux Consciences* by Paul Anthelme. Starring: Montgomery Clift, Anne Baxter, Karl Malden, Brian Aherne, O. E. Hasse.

DIAL M FOR MURDER (a Warner Brothers-First National Picture production/1954)
Directed and produced by Alfred Hitchcock. Screenplay by Frederick Knott, based on his play. Starring: Grace Kelly, Ray Milland, Robert Cummings, Anthony Dawson, John Williams.

REAR WINDOW (Paramount Pictures/1954)
Directed and produced by Alfred Hitchcock. Screenplay by John Michael Hayes, based on the short story by Cornell Woolrich. Starring James Stewart, Grace Kelly, Thelma Ritter, Wendell Corey, Raymond Burr, Judith Evelyn.

TO CATCH A THIEF (Paramount Pictures/1955)
Directed and produced by Alfred Hitchcock. Screenplay by John Michael Hayes, based on the novel by David Dodge. Starring: Cary Grant, Grace Kelly, Jessie Royce Landis, John Williams, Brigitte Auber, Charles Vanel.

THE TROUBLE WITH HARRY (Paramount Pictures/1955)
Directed and produced by Alfred Hitchcock. Screenplay by John Michael Hayes, based on the novel by J. Trevor Story. Starring: Edmund Gwenn, John Forsythe, Shirley MacLaine, Mildred Natwick, Jerry Mathers.

THE MAN WHO KNEW TOO MUCH (Paramount Pictures/1956)
Directed and produced by Alfred Hitchcock. Associate producer: Herbert Coleman. Screenplay by John Michael Hayes, based on the story by Charles Bennett and D. B. Wyndham Lewis. Starring: James Stewart, Doris Day, Bernard Miles, Brenda De Banzie, Reggie Nalder, Daniel Gélin.

THE WRONG MAN (a Warner Brothers-First National Picture production/1956)
Directed and produced by Alfred Hitchcock. Associate producer: Herbert Coleman. Screenplay by Maxwell Anderson and Angus McPhail, based on the story by Maxwell Anderson. Starring: Henry Fonda, Vera Miles, Anthony Quayle, Doreen Lang, Esther Minciotti, Harold J. Stone.

VERTIGO (Paramount Pictures/1958)
Directed and produced by Alfred Hitchcock. Associate producer: Herbert Coleman. Screenplay by Alec Coppel and Samuel Taylor, based on the novel *D'Entre Les Morts* by Pierre Boileau and Thomas Narcejac. Starring: James Stewart, Kim Novak, Barbara Bel Geddes, Tom Helmore, Henry Jones, Ellen Corby.

NORTH BY NORTHWEST (an M-G-M Picture/1959)
Directed and produced by Alfred Hitchcock. Associate producer: Herbert Coleman. Screenplay by Ernest Lehman. Starring: Cary Grant, Eva Marie Saint, James Mason, Jessie Royce Landis, Leo G. Carroll, Martin Landau.

PSYCHO (Paramount Pictures/1960)
Directed and produced by Alfred Hitchcock. Screenplay by Joseph Stefano, based on the novel by Robert Bloch. Starring: Anthony

Perkins, Janet Leigh, Vera Miles, John Gavin, Martin Balsam, Patricia Hitchcock, John McIntire, Lurene Tuttle, Simon Oakland, Frank Albertson, Vaughn Taylor.

THE BIRDS (a Universal Release/1963)
Directed and produced by Alfred Hitchcock. Screenplay by Evan Hunter, based on the short story by Daphne Du Maurier. Starring: Tippi Hedren, Rod Taylor, Jessica Tandy, Suzanne Pleshette, Veronica Cartwright, Doreen Lang.

MARNIE (a Universal Release/1964)
Directed and produced by Alfred Hitchcock. Screenplay by Jay Presson Allen, based on the novel by Winston Graham. Starring: Tippi Hedren, Sean Connery, Diane Baker, Louise Latham, Martin Gabel, Bob Sweeney, Mariette Hartley, Bruce Dern.

TORN CURTAIN (a Universal Release/1966)
Directed and produced by Alfred Hitchcock. Screenplay by Brian Moore. Starring: Paul Newman, Julie Andrews, Lila Kedrova, David Opatoshu, Ludwig Donath, Tamara Toumanova.

TOPAZ (a Universal Release/1969)
Directed and produced by Alfred Hitchcock. Associate producer: Herbert Coleman. Screenplay by Samuel Taylor, based on the novel by Leon Uris. Starring: Frederick Stafford, John Forsythe, Dany Robin, John Vernon, Claude Jade, Philippe Noiret, Michel Piccoli, Karin Dor.

FRENZY (a Universal Release/1972)
Directed and produced by Alfred Hitchcock. Screenplay by Anthony Shaffer, based on the novel *Goodbye Piccadilly, Farewell Leicester Square* by Arthur Labern. Starring: Jon Finch, Barry Foster, Barbara Leigh-Hunt, Anna Massey, Alec McCowen, Vivien Merchant, Billie Whitelaw, Clive Swift, Bernard Cribbins.

FAMILY PLOT (a Universal Picture/1976)
Directed and produced by Alfred Hitchcock. Screenplay by Ernest Lehman, based on the novel *The Rainbird Pattern* by Victor Canning. Starring: Bruce Dern, Barbara Harris, William Devane, Karen Black, Ed Lauter, Nicholas Colasanto.

Bibliography

Books

Anobile, Richard A., ed. *Alfred Hitchcock's PSYCHO.* New York, Universe Books, 1974.

Bankhead, Tallulah. *My Autobiography.* New York: Harper & Brothers, 1952.

Barbier, Philippe, and Jacques Moreau. *Album Photos: Alfred Hitchcock.* Paris: Pac, 1985.

Bazin, André. *Le Cinéma de la Cruauté.* Paris: Flammarion, 1987.

Bellour, Raymond. *L'Analyse du Film.* Paris: Editions Albatros, 1979.

Behlmer, Rudy. *Memo from David O. Selznick.* New York: Viking, 1972.

Bjorkman, Stig, Jonas Sima and Trosten, Mams. *Bergman on Bergman* Translated by Paul Britten. New York: Simon & Schuster. 1970/1973.

Brill, Leslie. *The Hitchcock Romance, Love and Irony in Hitchcock's Films.* Princeton, N.J.: Princeton University Press. 1988.

Brown, Bryan. *The Alfred Hitchcock Movie Quiz Book.* New York: Perigee Books, 1986.

Brown, Peter Harry. *Kim Novak, Reluctant Goddess.* New York: St. Martin's Press, 1986.

Callan, Michael Feeny. *Sean Connery, His Life and Films.* London: W. H. Allen, 1983.

Carey, Cary. *Marlon Brando: The Only Contender.* New York: St. Martin's Press, 1985.

Cotten, Joseph. *An Autobiography; Vanity Will Get You Nowhere.* New York: Mercury House, 1987.

Cronyn, Hume. *A Terrible Liar; Hume Cronyn. A Memoir.* New York: William Morrow, 1991.

DeMille, Cecil B. *The Autobiography of Cecil B. DeMille.* Edited by Donald Hayne. Englewood Cliffs: N.J.: Prentice Hall, 1959.

Dentlebaum and Leland Poague, eds. *A Hitchcock Reader.* Iowa State University Press, 1986.

Dietrich, Marlene. *Marlene Dietrich.* New York: Grove Press, 1987.

Douchet, Jean. *Hitchcock.* L'Herne, 1967, Paris: New Edition, 1985.

Ducout, Françoise. *Les Fantômes de Grand Central.* Paris: Pierre Hovay, 1988.

Durgnat, Raymond. *The Strange Case of Alfred Hitchcock, or The Plain Man's Hitchcock.* Cambridge, Mass.: MIT Press, 1974.

Estève, Michel, ed. *Alfred Hitchcock.* Paris: Minard, 1971.

Finler, Joel W. *Hitchcock in Hollywood.* New York: Continuum Publishing Group, 1992.

Freeman, David. *The Last Days of Alfred Hitchcock.* New York: Overlook Press, 1984.

Gielgud, John. *Gielgud, An Actor of His Time;* in collaboration with John Miller and John Powell. New York: Clarkson N. Potter, Inc., 1979.

Goldman, William. *Adventures to the Screen Trade.* New York: Warner Books, 1983.

Halley, Michael. *The Alfred Hitchcock Album.* Englewood Cliffs, N.J.: Prentice Hall, 1981.

Halliwell, Leslie. *Halliwell's Filmgoer's and Video Viewer's Companion, 9th ed.* New York: Harper & Row, 1990.

———— *The Filmgoer's Book of Quotes.* London: Hart-Davis, MacGibbon, 1973.

Harris, Robert A., and Michael S. Lasky. *The Films of Alfred Hitchcock.* New York: Citadel press, 1976.

Harris, Warren G. *Cary Grant: A Touch of Elegance.* Garden City, L.I.: Doubleday, 1987.

Haver, Donald. *David O. Selznick's Hollywood.* New York: Bonanza Books, 1980.

Head, Edith, and Paddy Calistro. *Edith Head's Hollywood.* New York: E.P. Dutton, 1983.

Hotchner, A. E. *Doris Day, Her Own Story.* New York: William Morrow, 1976.

Humphries, Patrick. *The Films of Alfred Hitchcock.* Greenwich, Conn.: Brom Books, 1986.

Kapsis, Robert E. *Hitchcock: The Making of a Reputation.* University of Chicago Press, 1992.

Kazan, Elia. *Eliz Kazan: A Life.* New York: Alfred A. Knopf, 1988.

Leff, Leonard J. *Hitchcock and Selznick.* New York: Weidenfeld & Nicolson, 1987.

Leitch, Thomas M. *Find and Director and Other Hitchcock Games.* University of Georgia Press, 1991.

McGillian, Pat. *Backstory; Interviews with Screenwriters of Hollywood's Golden Age.* Berkeley & Los Angeles, London: University of California Press, 1986.

McShane, Frank. *The Life of Raymond Chandler.* E. P. Dutton, 1976.

Modelski, Tania. *The Women Who Knew Too Much; Hitchcock and Feminist Theory.* New York: Methuen, 1988.

Montcoffe, Francis. *Fenêtre sur Cour.* Paris: Nathan, 1990.

Morella, Joe, and Edward Z. Epstein. *Paul and Joanne: A Biography of Paul Newman and Joanne Woodward.* Delacorte, 1988.

Morley, Sheridan. *James Mason, Odd Man Out.* New York: Harper & Row, 1989.

Olivier, Laurence. *Laurence Olivier: On Acting.* New York: Simon & Schuster, 1986.

Perry, George. The Films of Alfred Hitchcock. New York: Dutton/Vista, 1965.

———— *Hitchcock.* Garden City, N.Y.: Doubleday, 1975.

Phillips, Gene D. *Alfred Hitchcock.* Boston: Twayne Publishing, 1984.

Powell, Michael. *Michael Powell: A Life in Movies and Art.* London: Heinemann, 1986.

Price, Theodore. *Hitchcock and Homosexuality.* Scarecrow Press, 1992.

Raubicheck, Walter, and Walter Srebnick, eds. *Hitchcock's Rereleased Films; From Rope to Vertigo.* Wayne, Neb.: Wayne State University Press, 1991.

Rebello, Stephen. *Alfred Hitchcock and the Making of Psycho.* New York: Dembner Books, 1990.

Rohmer, Eric, and Claude Chabrol. *Hitchcock: The First 44 Films.* New York: Frederick Ungar, 1979.

Rothman, William. *Hitchcock: The Murderous Gaze.* Cambridge, Mass.: Harvard University Press, 1982.

Ryall, Tom. *Alfred Hitchcock and the British Cinema.* Urbana, Ill.: University of Illinois Press, 1986.

Schoell, William. *Stay Out of the Shower.* New York: Dembner Books, 1985.

Sharff, Stephan. *Alfred Hitchcock's High Vernacular.* New York: Columbia University Press, 1991.

Simone, Sam P. *Hitchcock as Activist; Politics and the War Films.* UMI Research Press, 1985.

Simsolo, Noel. *Alfred Hitchcock.* Paris: Seghers, 1979.

Sinyard, Neil. *The Films of Alfred Hitchcock.* New York: Galley Books, 1986.

Smith, Steven C. *A Heart at Fire's Center; the Life and Music of Bernard Herrmann.* Berkeley: University of California Press, 1991.

Spada, James. *Grace: The Secret Life of a Princess*. New York: Dolphin Books, 1987.

Spotto, Donald. *The Dark Side of Genius: The Life of Alfred Hitchcock*. Boston: Little, Brown, 1983.

_____ *The Art of Alfred Hitchcock: 50 Years of His Motion Pictures*. New York: Anchor Books, 1976; new ed., 1992.

Tabori, George. *Monty*. Arbor House, 1977.

Taylor, John Russell. *Hitch: The Life and Times of Alfred Hitchcock*. New York: Pantheon Books, 1978.

Truffaut, François. *Hitchcock/Truffaut*. New York: Simon & Schuster, 1983.

Villien, Bruno. *Hitchcock*. Paris: Rivages, 1985.

Weiss, Elisabeth. *The Silent Scream: Alfred Hitchcock's Soundtrack*. Associated University Presses, Inc., 1982.

Wood, Robin. *Hitchcock's Films Revisited*. New York: Columbia University Press, 1989.

Yacowar, Maurice. Hitchcock's British Films. Hamden, Conn.: Archon Books, 1977.

Zimmer, Jacques. *Alfred Hitchcock*. Paris: J'ai Lu, 1988.

Zizek, Slavoj, ed. *Tout ce que Vous Avez Toujours Voulu Savoir sur Lacan sans Jamais Oser le Demander à Hitchcock*. Paris: Navarin, 1980.

Periodicals

Anonymous. "Hitchcock." *Life*, magazine 20 November 1939.

Anonymous. "Alfred Hitchcock: Director and Extra." *New York Times*, 28 October 1945.

Anonymous. "The Star in Hitch's Heaven." *News Review.* 10 March 1949.

Anonymous. "Hitchcock on a Train." New York *Daily News*, 27 November 1950.

Anonymous. "Hitchcock Chuckles Out of Disappearance." *Los Angeles Times*, 29 December 1955.

Anonymous. "Hitchcock Speaking." *Cosmopolitan*, October 1956.

Anonymous. "Hitchcock Gives View on Sex." *Los Angeles Times*, 21 December 1959.

Anonymous. "Hitchcock on the Tricks of his Trade." *People*, 20 May 1974.

Anonymous. "Hitchcock Shrugs Off Crippling Illnesses at 80 to Keep Working on Another Thriller." *The Star*, 5 February 1980.

Belcher, Jerry. Master of Suspense Dead at 80. *Los Angeles Times*, 29 April 1980.

Blume, Mary. "Hitchcock Keeps His Cool on *Frenzy* Film Set." *Los Angeles Times*, 2 January 1972.

Cinefantastique Special Issue. "The Birds." Fall 1980.

Cinefantastique Special Issue. "Psycho." 10 October 1986.

Davis, Ivor. "Alfred Hitchcock Abhors Violence; Prefers Violence." *Los Angeles Times,* 7 September 1969.

Diehl, Digby. "Q & A, Alfred Hitchcock." *Los Angeles: Herald Examiner,* 25 June 1972.

Flatley, Guy. "I Tried to Be Discreet With That Nude Corpse." *New York Times,* 18 June 1972.

Goodman, Ezra. "The World Is Now With Hitchcock." *New York Herald Tribune,* 5 April 1942.

_____ Untitled. New York *Daily News,* 29 March 1950.

Hitchcock, Alfred. "The Woman Who Knows Too Much." *McCalls,* March 1956.

Hitchcock, Alma, as told to Elizabeth Sherrill. *Everyone's Family Circle,* June 1958.

Hildebrand, Harold. "Hitchcock Himself in Suspense 15 Years." *Los Angeles Herald Examiner,* 26 July 1959.

Schumack, Murray. "Hitchcock Insists Plot Is Vital to Suspense." *New York Times,* 12 February 1961.

Hopper, Hedda. "Alfred's Solution to Actor Problem." *Los Angeles Times,* 29 April 1962.

Heffenan, Harold. "Hitch Views the Stars." *Milwaukee Journal.* 3 March 1963.

Hitchcock, Alfred and Dr. Fredric Wertham. "Redbook Dialogue" *Redbook,* April 1963.

Hitchcock, Patricia, as told to Marya Saunders. "My Dad, the Jokester." *Citizen News,* 7 July 1963.

Hitchcock, Alma, as told to Martin Abramson. My Husband Alfred Hitchcock Hates Suspense." *Coronet,* August 1964.

Hodenfield, Chris. "Muuuurder by the Babbling Brook." *Rolling Stone,* 29 July 1976.

Heydt, Bruce. "The Master." *British Heritage,* June-July 1991.

Knight, Arthur. "Killing Some Time With Alfred Hitchcock." *Los Angeles Times,* 23 July 1972.

_____"Conversation With Alfred Hitchcock." *Oui,* 2 February 1973.

Kendall, Bob. "Hitchcock Speaks Out." *Hollywood Studios,* June 1976.

Lehman, Ernest. "Hitch." *American Film.* 29 April 1980.

Mc Clay, Howard. " 'Fans Like Anxiety,' Hitchcock." New York *Daily News,* 20 July 1954.

Martin, Pete. "I Call on Alfred Hitchcock." *Saturday Evening Post,* 27 July 1957.

Maslin, Janet. "Alfred Hitchcock." *Boston After Dark,* 13 June 1972.

McBride, Joseph. "Nothing Will Ever Stop Hitch." *Variety,* 28 October 1975.

Miller, Mark Crispin. "In Memoriam: Alfred Hitchcock." *New Republic,* 26 July 1980.

Ruark, Robert C. Untitled. *Citizen News,* 23 February 1950.

Rau, Neil. "Hitchcock Explains His 'Little Suspense Game.'" *Los Angeles Herald Examiner,* 24 June 1956.

Reed, Rex. "Master of the Macabre." *South Land Sunday.* 30 July 1972.

Scheca, Philip K. "Hitch Your Mystery to Star, But Let Your Audience In on It." *Los Angeles Times,* 15 February 1953.

Schumach, Murray. "Hitchcock Insists Plot Is Vital to Suspense." *New York Times,* 12 February 1961.

Smith, Cecil. "Tea and Empathy With Hitchcock." *Los Angeles Times,* 24 September 1962.

Whitcomb, Jon. "Master of Mayhem." *Cosmopolitan,* October 1959.

Warhol, Andy, and Pat Hackett. "Hitchcock." *Interview Magazine,* July 1974.

Wakarska. "Hitch at the Helm." *Village Voice,* 8 September 1975.

Wixen, Joan. "Alfred Hitchcock: The Man Behind the Profile." *Family Circle,* May-June 1976.

Hitchcock on Video

(The asterisk indicates film titles also available on laserdisc. The name of the releasing company is mentioned if different from that of the videotape.)

The Lodger (Hollywood Select Video)

Easy Virtue (Hollywood Select Video)

The Ring (Hollywood Select Video)

Champagne (Hollywood Select Video)

The Manxman (Hollywood Select Video)

Blackmail (Hollywood Select Video; special laserdisc edition featuring interview with Charles Bennet and audio commentary read by Stuart Birnbaum and written by Laurent Bouzereau. Also featured, sound screen test and Hitchcock rehearsing on the set/The Criterion Collection)

Juno and the Paycock (Hollywood Select Video)

Murder! (Hollywood Select Video)

Number Seventeen (Hollywood Select Video)

Rich and Strange (Hollywood Select Video; also available on laserdisc/Image Entertainment)

The Man Who Knew Too Much (Hollywood Select Video; also available on laserdisc/Image Entertainment)

The 39 Steps (Hollywood Select Video; also available on laserdisc/The Criterion Collection)

Secret Agent (Hollywood Select Video; also available on laserdisc/The Criterion Collection)

Sabotage (Hollywood Select Video; also available on laserdisc/The Criterion Collection

Young and Innocent (Hollywood Select Video; also available on laserdisc/The Criterion Collection)

The Lady Vanishes (Hollywood Select Video; also available on laserdisc/The Criterion Collection

Jamaica Inn (Hollywood Select Video)

Rebecca (CBS/Fox Co.; CLV version and CAV special edition featuring audio commentary by Leonard J. Leff, rare screen tests, Academy Award footage, excerpts from Truffaut's interview with Hitchcock, and other material also available on laserdisc/The Criterion Collection)

Foreign Correspondent (Warner Home Video)★

Mr. and Mrs. Smith (The Nostalgia Merchant; also available on laserdisc/Image Entertainment)

Suspicion (The Image Merchant/Colorized version: Turner Home Entertainment; also available on laserdisc/Image Entertainment)

Saboteur (MCA Home Video)★

Shadow of a Doubt (MCA Home Video)★

Lifeboat (CBS/Fox Co.)★

Spellbound (CBS/Fox Co.)★

Notorious (CBS/Fox Co.; CLV version and CAV special edition featuring audio commentary by Rudy Behlmer, theatrical trailer, production photos, and other material on the film also available on laserdisc/The Criterion Collection)

The Paradine Case (CBS/Fox Co.)

Rope (MCA Home Video)★

Under Capricorn (Vidamerica; also available on laserdisc/Image Entertainment)

Stage Fright (Warner Home Video)★

Strangers on a Train (Warner Home Video)★

I Confess (Warner Home Video)★

Dial M For Murder (Warner Home Video)★

Rear Window (MCA Home Video)★

To Catch a Thief (Paramount Home Video)★

The Trouble With Harry (MCA Home Video)★

The Man Who Knew Too Much (MCA Home Video)

The Wrong Man (Warner Home Video)★

Vertigo (MCA Home Video)★

North by Northwest (M-G-M/UA Home Video-Turner Home Entertainment; M-G-M/UA Home Video-Turner Home Entertainment/laserdisc-letterbox format; CLV version and CAV/letterbox special edition featuring interview with Hitchcock, storyboards, trailer, and other material on the film also available on laserdisc/The Criterion Collection)

Psycho (MCA Home Video)★

The Birds (MCA Home Video)★

Marnie (MCA Home Video)★

Torn Curtain (MCA Home Video)★

Topaz (MCA Home Video★; the laserdisc features the two alternate endings that Hitchcock shot for the film but were never used.)

Frenzy (MCA Home Video)★

Family Plot (MCA Home Video)★

Alfred Hitchcock Presents (MCA Home Video; the videotape features three episodes of the TV series directed by Hitchcock: "Lamb to the Slaughter," "The Case of Mr. Pelham," "Banquo's Chair"; the laserdisc also features an episode entitled "Back for Christmas.")

Also on tape:

The American Film Institute Life Achievement Awards

Alfred Hitchcock (Worldvision Home Video, Inc. laserdisc: Image Ent.)

Hitchcock Trailers (SF Rush Video)

ABOUT THE AUTHOR

Laurent Bouzereau is the author of *The De Palma Cut*. He wrote a commentary featured on an analog audio track for special laserdisc editions of Alfred Hitchcock's *Blackmail* and Brian De Palma's *Carrie*. Bouzereau also did the new subtitle adaptations of eight films by François Truffaut. Bouzereau was born in Paris and lives in Los Angeles.

NOTE

Every effort has been made to properly credit those stills, publicity shots, and other photographs included herein. Any errors are purely unintentional and, if brought to our attention, will be corrected for future editions. All stills are from the author's private collection.

Index